THE
DEMING
VISION

THE DEMING VISION:

SPC/TQM for Administrators

Gary Fellers

ASQC Quality Press
Milwaukee, Wisconsin

The Deming Vision: SPC/TQM for Administrators
Gary Fellers

Library of Congress Cataloging-in-Publication Data

Fellers, Gary
    The Deming vision: SPC/TQM for administrators/Gary Fellers.
        p.   cm.
    Includes bibliographical references and index.
    ISBN 0-87389-128-7
    1. Total quality management. 2. Deming, W. Edwards (William Edwards).
    3. Process Control — Statistical methods. I. Title.
HD62.15.F45 1992
658.5'62 — dc20   91-31583
                                                             CIP

1098765432

ISBN 0-87389-128-7

Acquisitions Editor: Jeanine L. Lau
Production Editor: Mary Beth Nilles
Marketing Administrator: Susan Westergard
Set in Garamond Book Condensed by Zahn-Klicka-Hill. Cover design by Laura Bober.
Printed and bound by Book Crafters.

For a free copy of the ASQC Quality Press Publications Catalog, including ASQC membership information, call 800-248-1946.

 Printed on Recycled Paper

Printed in the United States of America

ASQC
Quality Press
611 East Wisconsin Avenue
Milwaukee, Wisconsin 53202

CONTENTS

PREFACE

Careful analysis and re-study of the works of W. Edwards Deming inspired the writing of this book. Many years of helping consulting clients and students put Dr. Deming's concepts into practice have provided the varied examples of this work. This book differs from most previous writings on the Deming philosophy in three ways. First, there are many more actual numerical examples. The author was present when these cases happened. Second, the main thrust pertains to administrative examples. There are, however, some manufacturing case studies. Third, the major emphasis is not just quality improvement, even though there are some guidelines included to help a firm improve quality. An equal emphasis is given to productivity, costs, job satisfaction, and administrative efficiency.

There is no quick fix; a firm cannot "install" knowledge. It takes time, and for most firms what is required is a near complete changing of administrative management practices. To quote Albert Einstein, "The significant problems we face cannot be solved at the same level of thinking we were at when we created them." The intent of this book is not to make the reading of Dr. Deming's book, *Out of the Crisis,* unnecessary, but to further aid your thinking as it pertains to your firm's transformation. An implementation strategy is provided. The transition needed by the typical firm is profound. This undertaking is by all means not for the meek.

ACKNOWLEDGMENTS

My desire for knowledge can be attributed to my parents, George and Jackie Fellers. The clarity of mind that made this project possible came from my wife, Pam Fellers. The clerical work, deserving great praise, was performed by Acetra McWilliams. The technical accuracy can be attributed to the industry reviewers:

Mr. David Ashcraft, Temple-Inland
Mr. W. C. Cole, Temple-Inland
Dr. Mary Mobley, Augusta College
Mr. Barry Norton, Helena Chemical Company
Mr. Joe Count, Kimberly-Clark
Ms. Sherry Young, University Hospital
Mr. Bill Bern, Weyerhaeuser
Mr. Frank Gardner, International Paper
Mr. John Hollowell, ASH Insurance Associates
Mr. Richard Lawson, DSM Chemicals
Ms. Angela Lanzafame, ASH Insurance Associates
Dr. Mike McDonald, Georgia Southern University

All the profound knowledge resulted from the teachings of Dr. W. Edwards Deming. The examples are all real and belong to my consulting clients. All the mistakes belong to the author. Except where noted, the author was present to experience the occurrences about which you read.

INTRODUCTION

Statistics show that since 1965 the international competitiveness of the United States has fallen. As an example, in 1950 this country produced 50 percent of the world's steel; now it produces only 10 percent. On the other hand, there are data to show that what has happened is mostly a normal economic adjustment that followed World War II. The United States produced approximately 25 percent of the world national product (WNP) before 1940. During the 1950s, as the rest of the world rebuilt after the war, the United States share of the WNP temporarily rose to almost 45 percent. Now it is back to about 25 percent, its equilibrium prewar level. This present percentage still is quite remarkable considering that only five percent of the world's population is in the United States.

The macroeconomic forces, including normal postwar readjustments or excessive United States interest rates, certainly were a factor to explain why the United States output growth per capita was a meager 1.9 percent during the 1950 to 1984 period, whereas it was 5.7 percent for Japan and 4.2 percent for West Germany. However, the 1990 study by the MIT Commission on Industrial Productivity found consistent micro forces, or management misconceptions, within typical U.S. firms that were perceived to account for about 85 percent of our decline, with only 15 percent attributed to macro forces.[1]

When the "NBC White Paper: If Japan Can Do It, Why Can't We?" aired in June 1980, a philosophical gentleman named W. Edwards Deming made some surprising and profound statements about the *Deadly Diseases* of the United States, the *14 Points* to help cure these diseases, and typical *Obstacles* that hinder our progress. To make his comments even more challenging, he stated that a deep understanding of statistics would enlighten employees and managers to help them make the transition. Now, 10 years later, there are many positive signs pertaining to the "transition" that Dr. Deming referred to in his conversations. However, the typical U.S. firm still "has" most of the Deadly Diseases and, believe it or not, a bottom-line profitability of only 50 to 65 percent of what it eventually could be. It is unlikely that any firm will "double" its net profit by adopting the Deming philosophy because of the human tendency toward private agendas, and thus suboptimization. The gap can certainly be closed in all cases as teamwork improves.

This book offers some new insight into the previous writings on the Deming philosophy, but in no way should it preclude one from reading any, or all, of the books listed in the reference section, especially Dr. Deming's great work *Out of the Crisis*. I have had an opportunity to see hundreds of examples of managers' confusions and disbeliefs about Dr. Deming's work. The typical executive has not had (or taken) the time to study Dr. Deming's principles over many years of reflective endeavors and across many books and seminars. Thus, what is typically missing in the executive's mind is the vision, the unifying theory, or the "glue" that pulls it all together. The intent of this book is to provide this unifying theory. The top executive needs to be able to show the rest of the firm that he or she has taken a "follow me, I have a road map" approach, versus the often benign "I support you all the way" image. Management support is good; however, executive example is what is needed to make the transition that Dr. Deming and others were part of in Japan after World War II. Top management must have the vision, the unifying theory to provide the initial examples for the firm.

There is a consistent theory relating to statistical process control (SPC) that explains the Deadly Diseases and how the implementation of the 14 Points will provide a "cure." Without an appreciation of the theory, fragmented implementation of individual parts of the 14 Points will be helpful, but the firm will not make the total transition and the resulting incremental profitability will be less than one-third what it could be. This book provides an easy-to-understand discussion of the theory that will enable the reader to see how and why it all works. Those who learn the principles well will be able to assume the role of visionary leader.

Please peruse the reference list at this point. To quote Isaac Newton, "If I have been able to see farther than others, it was because

I have stood on the shoulders of giants." Great works of previous writers and constant challenging of industrial clients and students have provided you with this book. Takeo Fujisawa, cofounder of Honda, once stated, "Japanese and American managers are 95 percent the same and differ in all important respects."[2] We often work so hard to do so poorly in this country. This book primarily addresses the "all important respects" that Mr. Fujisawa mentions. American managers are, in some ways, better trained and are equally motivated compared to any leaders in the world. In most cases, however, we are missing the unifying theory that will seem so simple once having read this book. All the examples are real and all the generalizations are based on first-hand, business experience.

Thanks, Dr. Deming, for providing a unifying theory of management. Johann W. von Goethe once said, "Everything has been thought before, but the problem is to think of it again." It is with great hope that this book will enable the readers to "think of it again." Anywhere an apparent missing citation for a knowledgeable fact exists, the readers can assume that it came from Dr. Deming's statements during a seminar.

Many management gurus are making a fortune expounding and preaching about the image that the American manager does not care about quality. This fact is no longer true. It is that they simply know not what to do to improve. The "system" is preventing progress. This book will help these managers.

1
HOW COULD WE HAVE KNOWN?

One could skip this chapter and still gain some insight on how to implement the Deming philosophy. Implementation, however, would be a frustrating experience because of your lack of patience with your less insightful coworkers. In many cases, in the beginning, it will seem somewhat like "showing a wristwatch to a pig" when you start explaining to seasoned executives that their sacred approaches to management are actually counterproductive to the long-range goals of the firm. You will understand how statistics can explain how things are often not what they seem, but your associates will not understand this in the beginning. An understanding on your part of how these archaic approaches to management evolved and how this could have happened will enable you to appreciate Dr. Deming's famous statement, "How could they have known?" Knowing the historical perspective will enhance your patience and nurturing ability, both of which are needed to make the Deming transformation. Dr. Deming has stated many times that experience teaches us nothing without theory. The problem with enhancing long-term business success with the Deming philosophy is that the theory is related to the scary topic of statistics. The upcoming chapters will remove this fear and give you a working model to start your firm's transition.

To be discussed in detail later, many of the Deadly Diseases of

U.S. business managers are manifested as the short-term, bottom-line approaches to operating versus a long-term process orientation where it is understood that the proper inputs will yield the desirable output. The evolution of this "tail wagging the dog" mentality was a natural and seemingly proper response to the post World War II situation. There were few dissenters at the time, except Dr. Deming, who was ignored in the U.S. Most of the rest of the industrialized world was devastated during the war. Consequently, the quantity demanded of U.S. product was greater than our ability to supply. The typical firm could sell practically anything. The issue of quality and productivity applied only as far as matching the domestic competition. The short-term, bottom-line approach seemed logical in the 1950s and 1960s. Why would anyone have done it differently? The concerns then were: keeping employees on their toes, worrying little about international competition, only matching the domestic competitors, making the quick money, getting the big bonus, getting a raise, getting promoted, etc. And why would one have done otherwise? Customers would buy practically anything expecting multiple return trips to the retailer to "get the bugs out." It was "buy American, or buy nothing" in most markets. Ouchi identified this generation of managers as "superstitiously trained."[3] Their training seemed to be applicable, and was at the time, but under a set of world economic conditions that were a fluke, would not last, and would never return. As an example of how bad we were, 30 years ago my father told me, "Never buy a new car; let someone else get the bugs out."

The problem that haunted us for 20 years, even after heightened awareness from the arrival of the first high-quality Datsun in California in 1969, was that the management approach of earlier decades had worked so well at the time, but was failing us now. (In comparison, blood-letting by a barber was an accepted treatment for disease in 1700!) By the time we sensed a big problem, around 1975, the young so-called "professional managers" of the 1950s were in the executive suite and were "superstitiously trained." How could they easily let go of management philosophies that made them rich and powerful? They understood that the rules of the game had changed as the rest of the world rebuilt after World War II, but they did not understand why international competitors were gaining on us so rapidly. Everyone tried "a larger dose of the same medicine," and things generally got worse. The "prescription was wrong." But how could we have known?

The problem was that we treated a postwar historical accident like a permanent condition and got away with it for 20 years because the quantity demanded exceeded the quantity supplied. There were, however, other contributing and relating factors. For example, another historical freak incident involved Henry Ford II's inheritance in 1945 of a company in financial despair because his grandfather had hated accountants so badly.[4] To bring sense to the madness, Robert McNamara and his financial whiz kids were brought in and allowed to take over Ford Motor Company. This number-crunching business school crowd viewed everything from the ivory tower as a short-term, bottom-line situation and from its immediate impact on Wall Street. Product and process took a back seat to systems and financial controls. (Some of this was needed in 1945, but not so much and not for so long.) Because of the postwar historical accident, and only because of this occurrence, this management by-the numbers approach worked well at the time and got considerable press coverage. Hence, the "professional manager" was born and everybody wanted to be one. The smartest young people went to business school; or if they chose engineering, they gravitated toward defense or space industries. What resulted was approximately twice the number of engineers per capita in the labor force in Japan as in the United States. We were emphasizing financial controls in the 1960s, the Japanese and others were stressing process improvements, and by this time it was difficult for us to react. The Japanese grass roots attention to people, process, and product was like a momentous locomotive. It took a long time to get it moving, but it was not to be stopped very easily. Someone said once, and I think it was Bill Scherkenbach of General Motors, "Ten years do not 40 quarters make!" In other words, treat every quarter as an isolated and distinct period in which everyone has to prove himself or herself; and 10 years later others may have taken your business because you failed to begin projects that would not show a quick return. There was no long-term development of the process and product. This is what began happening to us in the years 1965 through 1975.

Even today 15 to 40 percent of factory costs for our manufactured product is from waste embedded in them.[5] The service sector is generally near the high side of this range. A large part of this problem is our failure to do the types of things that show a payback only over the years; in other words, our quarter-to-quarter or worse management by-the-numbers style. What is missing is generally an understanding of the Deming philosophy.

The superstitiously trained managers at first blamed most of their problems on the hourly workers. We have learned that this was an incorrect generalization. Yes, it may be true that the line operator failed to bolt the inside of your car door properly, but if you look deeper, you will find that the line could not be shut down for needed repairs and the foreman still meet his daily production quota. So hourly operators did the best they could in the system in which they worked. A ray of light was shed on the situation, however, when Japanese firms, with their different management philosophies, began opening plants in the United States, using American hourly workers, and achieved similar levels of quality and productivity as plants in Japan. The GM/Toyota joint venture in California is a case in point.

Things have begun to change. Ford Motor Company started its transformation in about 1981. As a result, its warranty costs are now down 45 percent, and Ford is saving $12,000,000 per day in operating costs that are attributable to the philosophies of W. Edwards Deming.[6] Anyone can temporarily save money by reducing overhead payroll. This was not from where these savings came. There will be many upcoming discussions of the types of things the people at Ford and other firms accomplished. Surely GM and Chrysler have been quick to make similar improvements. The point here is that the transformation has begun and that it pays big dividends. This is not to mention the fact that the truly important figures are usually "unknown and unknowable" (Deming's statement). Who can incorporate into their net present value capital budgeting formula the value of a satisfied customer, or the worth of an employee's feeling better about his or her job and workmanship? There will be many more examples of these "unknowns and unknowables" in this book. In all cases they are more important than what can be measured. In most cases five to 10 times more important. (Memorize this!)

The research from the book *The 100 Best Companies to Work for in America* has shown that the proper atmosphere can yield twice the corporate profitability, stock-price increases three times larger, with a total return to stockholders of over 17 percentage points higher than the average firm.[7] A deeper look into these "100 best firms" shows a general absence of the Deadly Diseases and the presence of most of the 14 Points. Hence, the Deming philosophy is in place. The founding fathers of these "best companies" created a culture that never let the Deadly Diseases take over. In 20 years practically every existing firm will be in the Deming mode. It will be the natural selection process of the survival of the fittest. Those who do not acquire and practice the vision will not exist in the long-term.

The model of the future is people orientation and teamwork, with the resulting synergies. (So what's new?) The confusing fact, as you will see, is that it is "what we do" that prevents the synergies. Peter Drucker once stated that most of what we do as managers prevents people from doing their jobs. The total is not greater than the sum of its parts (synergy). It's every man for himself. The superstitiously learned business tools of the 1950 to 1970 era that caused this predicament will be effectively discredited in this book. Chapter 2 contains the theory that binds this all together. There are certainly several examples that fit your situation exactly. Chapter 3 contains a brief overview of the Deming concept. The last five chapters treat each of the Five Deadly Diseases in detail. The theory, the why, and the how-to are included in each case.

The next chapter is the glue that binds the Deming philosophy together. Most practitioner hopefuls try to sidestep the enlightening theory and jump right into a to-do list, even though the basics are simple to understand. Even if the next chapter seems a bit long, do not get discouraged. The theory of this next chapter is interesting, is enlightening, and will give you the vision to patiently follow through to make the Deming transition. Go hug your kids, kiss your spouse, and turn the ringer on the phone to OFF. You are about to get totally immersed in the managerial vision of one of the most insightful gurus of the last 1,900 years, Dr. W. Edwards Deming. History is being rewritten; be an early visionary as the inevitable happens.

2
THE VISION

At this point most eager readers would expect lists of the Deadly Diseases, the 14 Points, and the Obstacles because that is what the Deming philosophy is perceived to be. However, you are not ready yet. Taking these brilliant lists as check-off items to be accomplished and eliminated from your desk may help to a small degree, but probably not very much in a lasting fashion (which is all that really counts). One must be "drenched" with the theory and examples and gain an understanding of variability to truly make the transition in his or her heart. This chapter makes it easy. Then, and only then, the executive will have the ability to tailor the guidelines to his or her environment, to motivate the subordinates, to explain the new, almost reversed management coaching philosophy, and to patiently follow through over the next three to five years. As Dr. Deming has taught, the transformation is not for the weak or the unstatistically trained. The theory of this chapter will help give you the understanding, strength, and motivation to make the transformation. Throwing money at massive training with no total understanding and road map by management accomplishes little. Granted, this may temporarily fool an ignorant customer, and at least it presents an image to the corporate bureaucrats that "we are doing something." To quote an industry sage, "Don't do something, just stand there!" In other words, grasp this theory of statistical process control (SPC) first, establish an immediate starting point to transform your own modus operandi, then ask your subordinates to follow you (do not simply state, "You have my support").

To expand on the theory, to be subsequently called "the Vision," there will be many examples in this chapter and others. Most of the examples are from administrative cases.

The "how-to" of implementing SPC on the manufacturing shop floor is well documented in literature and will not be discussed here at length. It is most simple, however, to begin here with a manufacturing example that will be extrapolated to the more general case.

If you can measure (record) data fairly accurately, you will always find that things do vary. And the word "always" means just that, "every time," unless someone is pressured to lie or sandbag. (Please note the word "accurately" in the first sentence of this paragraph.) When analyzing data, the immediate question is, "Do we react or not?" The longer-term question is, "What do we do to reduce this variability?" Accurate answers to these questions are based on a basic truism (this means no exceptions!): "When God created the universe, he made it inherently variable such that at times a process (or situation) can be right on target yet the measured results will vary somewhat during successive observations."

In other words, when measured (or observed) results seem to deviate, a basic determination is whether the difference away from target is a normal expected fluctuation or a variance large enough to warrant action. If the variation is normal, how can one further reduce it? You will see in a few moments, that failure to understand variability is the most basic shortcoming of American managers, perhaps their only widespread weakness. The main thrust of this book pertains to administrative examples; however, as a simple introductory example, consider a process that makes paper, supposedly of a thickness (caliper) of 0.1 millimeters (about the same as this page).

During a hypothetical five-minute period for this process when everything is exactly as it should be, assume that someone used a type of micrometer to take repeated thickness measurements. A tally of these data is shown in Figure 2.1. (For future examples the X's may

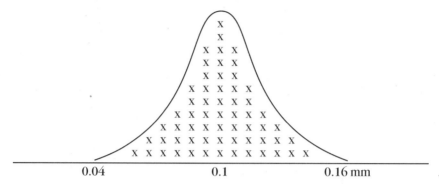

Figure 2.1   Common Cause Variability

be eliminated and represented by the bell-shaped curve.)

The point is that even when everything controllable about the process is right on target, there will still be some variability. This natural variability is called "common cause," since it is common to the system and cannot be removed or reduced by short-term conventional methods. Are there reasons behind it? Of course there are. It is not some sort of stochastic "white noise" from outer space that some theoretical statistician may inadvertently lead one to believe. The point is, however, that removal of common cause variability is never an easy, unidimensional, short-term process. It is "common" to the system at this level of technology, understanding, training, etc. Short-term pressure to "do better" will be useless or counterproductive as a means of removing common cause variability. From the previous example, the paper thickness varied from common cause that resulted from varying growth conditions of the trees, changing tap water temperature in the process, changing chemical strength from the vendors, etc., none of which were under the short-term control of the immediate paper mill employees. The common cause variability is not necessarily acceptable, but it is there and cannot be permanently removed by the local employees.

Obviously, when things go wrong at the local process, and this will happen eventually, there may be thickness measurements outside the limits to the left and right of the drawn-in bell-shaped curve in Figure 2.1. These occurrences are called "local faults" because they are beyond the common cause limits. There are likely local reasons the immediate employees can identify and repair. The upper and lower points of the bell-shaped curve are called control limits: upper control limit (UCL) and lower control limit (LCL). The center point is either the average ($\overline{X}$) or a feasible target. The data of Figure 2.1 can be redrawn as a time plot (Figure 2.2). This is called a control chart. Those responsible for constructing control charts must go to the references to learn the necessary technical facts.[8] The math is the easy part. Spreading the vision is what is difficult. The discussion has been somewhat freewheeling up to this point. However, the next short section involves an abrupt departure into a bit of statistical theory. Please tolerate the necessary change for several pages!

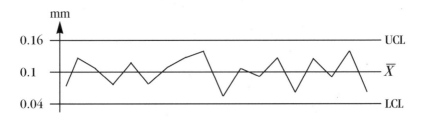

Figure 2.2   Control Chart

As a primer in SPC, assume that the product is immediately tested and the data are plotted in chronological sequence. If the points are randomly distributed about the center line ($\overline{X}$), the process is said to be in-control and no immediate action is warranted. The process is said to be stable. There is common cause variability, but this issue is a long-term concern, not a short-term local fault that an operator can immediately remedy. (More on reducing common cause later.) However, the process (situation) is "out-of-control," or has a local fault and thus something has changed, if one of the following occurs:

1. The last plotted point is outside UCL or LCL.
2. There is a long run of consecutive points above or below the center line (five to seven in a row are typical decision rules).

3. There are two-out-of-three consecutive points in the outer third zones of the chart.
4. There is an obvious trend or shift.

The rules may vary slightly in some cases. The point is that common cause is generally from many subtle sources and usually manifests itself as randomly and evenly distributed scatter about the average. Local faults are special causes (assignable causes) normally associated with the local issues, and can generally be remedied, or at least identified, by the local employees.

To summarize, there are two types of variability:

1. Common cause: Natural variability deeply rooted in the process (situation) that cannot be removed by typical means by the local employees in the short-term.
2. Local faults: Variability beyond the natural capabilities of the process (situation) that can generally be addressed by the local employees.

Why so much attention to the concept of variability? Failure to understand this concept is costing the typical large business firm an amount equal to approximately one-fourth to half their bottom line profit. The larger and more bureaucratic firms are typically at the higher end of this range. If you do not believe, read on! In fact, read on even if you do believe. The vision and the how-to will come eventually. Consider Figure 2.3 and assume that the process is still right on target (in-control), but an operator measures a sample with a thickness randomly away from target at 0.13 units. See the circled x.

The operator only sees this one specimen, which is a member of a large statistical population. If we have trained the operator well, he or she may have all the x's and the bell-shaped curve imaged in his or her head or a control chart; otherwise, there is no way to tell what the operator is thinking. In any event, there is one number in front of the operator, or maybe a few on a production log. Assume that the supervisor, not appreciating the concept of common cause, walks by and reminds the operator that the target is 0.1 millimeter for this

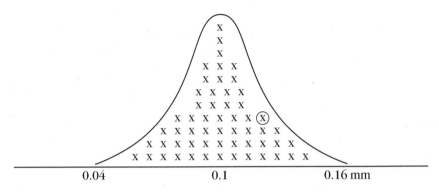

Figure 2.3   Common Cause Variability

product. The supervisor states, "Turn it down a bit." So what happens? As shown in Figure 2.4, he shifts the entire curve to the left. Then later, back to the right. Then back to the left again, ad nauseam!

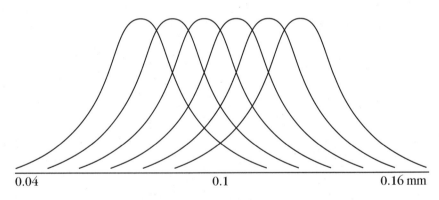

Figure 2.4   Example of Overcontrol

In practice, the typical operator obviously does not respond to every subtle deviation away from the point target (even though the author has seen a few cases of this). For the typical situation, however, when there is no statistical tool for reacting to deviations, the total variability will be generally 25 to 30 percent higher than

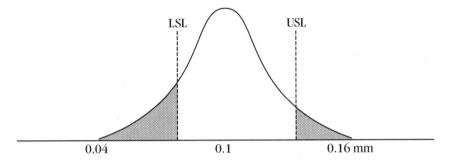

Figure 2.5   Incapable Process

necessary (cases of 80 percent higher are not uncommon). This is especially true when there is continual pressure to *do better*, along with no statistical vision.

In most business situations, when data are used to call attention to problems, management-imposed limits exist beyond which immediate action is warranted. In manufacturing, these limits are typically called specifications (specs). The real problem exists when the specs are not based on the natural process capabilities (UCL and LCL) as shown in Figure 2.5. The USL and LSL are upper and lower spec limits, respectively.

In this case there will be times when the process will be in-control but out-of-spec, and, surprisingly to some, should be temporarily left alone. (Even though the product should be sorted.) If, when controlling the process, the operator responds to the specs, for political reasons or innocently out of ignorance, the situation will become even more variable as shown in Figure 2.4. This leads to a basic truth that applies to everything, a manufacturing process, an office, your friends, or your spouse: "Demand more of a process in the short-term than it can yield, and matters will always get worse. More variability will result and people will get demoralized."

Referring back to Figure 2.5, assume that the specs are a commercial necessity. If this is the case, the common cause must be reduced so that the control limits are inside of the spec limits. This endeavor requires an approach fairly alien to many firms. The system, within which the employees must function, must be greatly improved. How to do this will be discussed shortly with an administrative example. Reducing common cause variability generally takes considerable time and resources, and is never totally (or typically even to a limited degree) within the capabilities of the local, most immediately visible employees. Upper management will have to do this, with the help of the local people. In all cases, the first steps for any quantifiable variable is to gather data (current or historical), create a control chart (which may be temporary), establish a plan to get it in-control and to classify the local faults, and then to organize to improve the system by reducing the common cause (as discussed later). An in-control system is defined as stable. It is nearly impossible to make long-lasting system improvements to an unstable situation. A real-time control system, an SPC chart, or whatever must be used to enable the employees to stamp out at least 95 percent of the local faults. Then it will be known that the local employees have done their jobs (or are doing them) and that further improvement will come only through explicit upper management actions. (Not just, "You have my support." Meaning: "Go solve my problems for me.") Those actions required of management will be identified shortly, but first a more general administrative example follows.

The chart in Figure 2.6 represents the administrative example of total plant waste in a carton factory. Four years of monthly data are shown. (As a technical note, the UCL and LCL are plus or minus three standard deviations from the average ($\overline{X}$). See Fellers for a complete discussion of the mathematics of SPC. It is sufficient here for the reader to merely understand that these control limits are the upper and lower boundaries resulting from natural process common cause.)

At a point in time represented by A, system improvements were made by management. The initial discussion here pertains to the three years to the left of point A. The control limits were established using the historical data, excluding the two out-of-control points (called outliers). The outliers, for known or unknown reasons, represented local faults that were not common to the system. Statistical theory tells us this. In this case, we were able to identify the

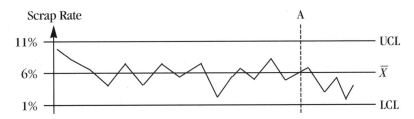

Figure 2.6   Plant Scrap Rate Over Time

local faults, which in reality were not caused by the local employees. So in this case, perhaps the phrase "assignable cause" may be preferable to local faults. The two weeks representing exceptionally high scrap rates were periods immediately preceding the infamous visits by the company president and his entourage of smiling faces. During these preceding weeks, everything was cleaned up from the "dark corners," baled, and weighed. Scrap was documented only when it was weighed. The point here is not to discredit executive visits. In fact, more first-hand contact would have been an improvement for this firm. The issue was that, pertaining to scrap rate, this plant was in-statistical-control. (An isolated point, one in 20, out of the limits even for unknown reasons does not classify a process as out-of-control.) Since in-control, the plant average ($\overline{X}$) or the plus or minus variability (UCL and LCL) was inherent to the system, and the local operators or foremen were powerless to do better in a lasting fashion. Trying harder was futile and even counterproductive at times. In fact, the three years prior to the data presented on the chart were exactly like the plot to the left of point A.

Before seeing the chart in the accountant's office, the plant manager commented that many of his efforts to jawbone the employees to "try harder" had been effective. He had been misled by a random fluctuation below the average (50 percent chance of this) or by unnatural, temporary reductions in scrap that could not be maintained for long because of intolerable tradeoffs. For example, slowing the process down temporarily causing production to be far below the plant expectations, inspecting less critically to reduce the scrap rate, employees working far above 100 percent pace to the point of exhaustion, etc. The point was that for over six years there had been no lasting improvement in scrap rate. Management's attempts had been useless, yet they were trying! The average and plus-or-minus limits had remained the same. Random system deviations (common cause) were responded to, but with demoralizing results. A compliment for being better than average was confusing because generally there was no assignable reason behind it, or the employees knew that they had been forced to do unnatural things that they found despicable or could not continue to repeat. The same system that produced the random highs yielded the temporary lows. A reprimand for being worse than average was even worse. The system common cause deviation had elicited criticism that they did not deserve. Since the chart (system) was in-control, there were no local faults that the plant personnel could have prevented.

The total Deming vision will be stated later. For now, here is a most important part of it:

> If you react to data in a non-statistical fashion and treat common cause variations as local faults, one of several bad consequences will occur. The best of the evils is that people ignore you, and many learn not to respect you. The employees may, however, do something unnatural or non-repeatable to "oil this week's squeaking wheel." This "knee-jerk" response is also confusing, demoralizing, and increases variability in the long-term (over-control). In any case, the creative spirit and energy of the employees is depleted. Then no long-term improvements are likely to occur.[9]

The "knee-jerk" response will be discussed many times in this book. For this firm, the constant badgering wore down the employees. Here is a typical scenario of "pep" talks they heard from the boss:

Week 1:   "Got to have less scrap. Only you people can do it!" (Scrap does go down, but production comes down.)

Week 2:	"Got to have more tonnage. Only you can do it!" (Quantity goes up. Quality goes down.)
Week 3:	"Customer complaints are up. Only you can stop this!" (Inspection is beefed up.)
Week 4:	"Too much downtime. Only you people can stop this!"
Weeks 5 to 50:	Ad nauseam! The creative spirit is gone. The employees are burned out.

In the context of the present scrap example, it is clear that each of the statements by management in response to a common cause fluctuation away from the average would likely have caused the scrap rate to plunge in the opposite direction, but not to stay there because of system tradeoffs.

As a review, local faults are those situations that are extraordinarily different and would generally yield a plotted point outside the limits on a control chart. In the absence of a control chart, local faults often manifest themselves as emergency situations. The immediate, local employees are usually able to handle these situations.

A system in this book is a collection of organizational (or functional) units for which only upper management has complete, effective control. System problems are those cross-functional issues we have learned to live with because no one person seemingly has complete control or knowledge of the situation. At times, we have grown so complacent that we are unaware of many of the systems issues.

Even in the absence of data, it is usually clear to a visionary person when extreme pressure has yielded unnatural, only temporary improvements. In these cases management previously viewed common causes as local faults. Hence, no lasting system improvements were made by management. When the manager leaves the scene, things go back to where they were. Overheard at a staff meeting: "I had the rework problem licked; however, when I went to Italy for six weeks to train on our new equipment, the employees quickly deteriorated back to where we were last year." Obviously there had been no system adjustments to yield permanent improvements. Does this example imply that management should have done nothing? Of course not —

the system average and variability about this average probably needed improving. These system improvements were possible, but required a rather explicit approach by upper management. As explained in a few pages, what was needed was the ad hoc formation of an interdepartmental think tank team to provide prioritized solutions to upper management, who were in advance sworn to take action on the recommendations. If in-statistical-control, what is happening is common to the system, there are few local faults that the apparently responsible operators and foremen can solve. Assuming that you had expert help in creating the control chart correctly, there are *no* exceptions to this fact. The local employees may know of a few of the system problems, but are powerless to do anything to remedy them. Consider the following general outline before returning to the previous example:

Local Faults

Variable out-of-control on a control chart
Likely short-term solution
Assignable cause probably readily identifiable
Subject for morning meeting
Solution mostly local
The old approach of "putting out fires" may be reasonably successful

System Problems

Variable in-control, but not good
Total and lasting solution not local: upper management is part of the answer (problem)
Long-term solution (one to five years is common)
Problems difficult to uncover — likely several contributing issues
Requires interdepartmental think tank approach
Not subject for morning meeting
Will demoralize if treated as local fault
The old approach of crisis management will not help (something different must be tried)

The important issue in cases like this scrap rate problem is for upper management to own up to the issue, to quit demoralizing the people, and to move on to the interdepartmental team to begin the long road to lasting system improvements. This Deming vision can enhance upper management patience, or for those who already have a gut feel for this issue, it can sanction his or her already effective style. In one of the worst, most hectic, high employee turnover factories the author ever consulted with, all the employees revealed that "the boss manages too closely." Every deviation from standard (quota, budget, average, etc.) is dealt with. It was confusing, discrediting, and energy draining. The knee-jerk response was omnipresent, and the more basic problem was that there was no energy available to begin the long-term process toward improving the system. Management mobility was a big problem. Like most unknowingly confused managers, this person was superstitiously trained, but extremely articulate. He could temporarily convince anyone that his modus operandi was good. Generally, an unenlightened person like this guy must develop a convincing style of articulation to survive and progress as the world and people's lives collapse around him. Be careful of these people and keep the Deming vision clear in your mind.

You will see in later chapters that this lack of statistical vision in the United States helped lead to many of the Deadly Diseases and superstitious learning. Consequently, many potentially creative and responsive employees have become "working stiffs," and this includes managers. Deming stated that only 2 percent of American managers truly love their work. Look at their faces when they leave the office at 5 P.M.! Douglas McGregor's Theory X/Theory Y concept led us to infer 25 years ago if we treat people like unmotivated children, they will in a self-fulfilling fashion be just that (Theory X). If you treat them as motivated, creative contributors, they will be just that (Theory Y). At his retirement ceremony, McGregor commented that he was all wrong. Now we understand why. In the normal case, management has constantly worn down and demoralized the employees by treating system problems as local faults — simply stated, asking for the impossible. Over time the world does begin to appear as Theory X. Then simply becoming a Theory Y manager with no deep statistical visions and road maps accomplishes little, except for a loss of confidence in human nature.

The most superstitiously trained, unvisionary managers generally have a very poor perception of human nature for this reason. Using the same scrap rate example (see Figure 2.6), the system capability was 6 percent plus or minus 5 percent. In other words, on the average, they cannot do better than 6 percent scrap, and it will randomly vary by 5 percentage points. Prior to point A on the chart, before the interdepartmental team and upper management had an impact, this meant that occasionally the weekly scrap rate would randomly be a low 1 to 2 percent. However, this was a freak, nonrepeatable occurrence when all those unknowns (common causes) stacked up just right. For example, no one was out sick, the room temperature and relative humidity were perfect, the raw materials were randomly better than average, the crabby quality assurance inspector was away at a seminar, all of which may not line up exactly right again for a year without drastic system changes beyond the employees' immediate control.

The executive vice president of this firm was a superstitiously trained guy. He wanted to "get this intolerable scrap issue off my desk." Not having the slightest idea of what to do, he looked at the last year's historical data (not a plot) and observed that 2.5 percent seemed feasible (even though we visionaries know that an isolated 2.5 percent month will occur because of seemingly random chance, but cannot be consistently maintained). (See Figure 2.6.) To quote him: "If you did it March of last year, why can't you repeat it?" It seemed to make sense to the corporate bureaucrats. You know the guys who know everything, but understand nothing! (Credit Lee Iacocca for this statement.) The vice president subsequently made this 2.5 percent scrap rate the plant managers' main performance objective for the upcoming year. (Remember, the system's natural average was 6 percent!) The connotation was "Meet this objective and your future looks good. Fail to meet it and I will think poorly of you." What happened? Nothing good! None of the plant managers met their objectives. None of them were stupid enough to drastically tamper with their technology and culture enough to try to respond by treating the system problems as local faults. Few of them were trained in the Deming vision, and thus could not make a persuasive argument to the superstitiously trained vice president, but from experience and common sense they knew what to (or not to) do. At the year-end plant managers' meeting they were told as a group, in effect, that they had failed the boss. Only the vice president did not understand. To be explained in great detail throughout this book, what was needed up-front a year earlier was a road map through masterful statistical guidance and an interdepartmental team. The vice president should have been trained and then shown the historical control chart, with an explicit and assertive message (by a guru) that what we have here is a system problem, not local faults. Asking the subordinates, once again, to do better at best accomplishes nothing. Remember the *zero defects* programs of the 1960s that sent the message that if we all do our best, things will get considerably better. Perhaps this worked momentarily at times for local faults; however, between 85 and 98 percent of business problems existing today are within the system, not easy enough for simply trying harder to help. This vice president needed guidance on assembling and running an interdepartmental team. The Hay Group Consulting firm reported from a survey of over a million employees that only 34 percent believed that management listened to their complaints.[10] Why? Generally, it was because there was no organized, scientific way for management to learn about system problems. Who wants to go into the bosses' office and tell him or her "If you want less scrap, you will have to make it happen. I am at the end of my rope!" The interdepartmental team and its inherent problem-solving tools are a way of accomplishing this objective.

The Interdepartmental Team

System problems are seldom unidimensional such that a single person or one functional specialist can solve the problem. For mature firms the typical remaining problems, often called by the exhausted insiders as "the nature of the beast," are not the type that a hero-hopeful can solve as he or she tries to draw the attention of the boss. This type of high-roller person does not function well on a project team, or generally anywhere these days, so keep them away from your people who hope to help you solve chronic system problems. One of Deming's 14 Points involves breaking down barriers among departments. In the typical firm bureaucratic dry rot has set in as functional specialists "stay within their box" on the organizational chart because of lack of vision, ignorance, a corporate culture to "stay on your own turf," or to concentrate on making the boss look good. For whatever reason, there is no synergy. In fact the opposite results in a very expensive fashion: The whole is less than the sum of its parts. True systems improvements often result from actions in the "white spaces" on the organizational chart. The interdepartmental teams used to identify and eliminate chronic problems are about the only proven technique that can systematically solve system issues, and at the same time improve the culture to remove some departmental boundaries. The following numbered procedure gives some guidelines on running an ad hoc interdepartmental team to solve problems when there are no emergencies, only system problems. Interdepartmental teams are referenced many times later in this book. Later, think back to these items (1 through 23) and the related discussions on problem solving coming up in several pages. Solving long-term, chronic systems problems requires doing "something different." This "something different" is likely items 1 through 23. See that the team players do not change the format toward their old modus operandi with which they are comfortable. Their old ways are not "something different." It will take discipline to overcome this NIH (not-invented-here) syndrome.

1. An interdepartmental team consists of four to eight people of varied skills across several functional departments. A typical team may be:

   Experienced operator(s) or clerks
   Process (manufacturing) engineer or accountant
   Superintendent or office manager
   Industrial Engineer or cost analyst
   R&D or technical service subject expert

   To quote Will Rogers, "Everybody is ignorant, only on different subjects."

2. It is advised to have one or more members from other locations, or at least one from a neutral department.

3. If a problem crosses departmental boundaries, there should be representatives from all areas.

4. There can be several specialists who are called in on an ad hoc basis. However, the people identified in item 1 are the "critical mass." Meetings are held only with 100 percent attendance by the "critical mass."

5. In the normal case, the team meets 90 minutes once per week. A "sacred" place should be identified. Hence, no pagers, no secretarial interruptions, no calls, etc. The meeting place should have several walls covered with writing board space (white boards preferred).

6. It is best to have a kickoff meeting with a meal, testimonials by upper managers, discussions on logistics, modus operandi, etc.

7. The tools of the team (to be discussed later) are:
   Brainstorming
   Cause and effect diagrams
   Pareto charts
   Flowcharts
   Trend charts
   Control charts
   Scatter diagrams
   Other statistical tools
   Common sense

8. There may be a need for recurring training for team members. A master must do this. No shortcuts here!

9. The team is formed by upper management who agrees to follow through with all recommendations, subject to budgetary constraints. Participation by members is preferably, but not necessarily, voluntary. Meetings are generally held during normal work hours.

10. Action items begin to emerge only near the end of the team endeavor. There will be meetings in the beginning that seem confusing. System problems are confusing and take months (years) to solve. By all means, do not always expect to generate a list of action items at every meeting. Do not give deadlines for solving global systems problems. Later, however, fragmented action items may be assigned reasonable due dates.

11. There will be many theoretical discussions, some of which will educate and enlighten, but do not lead to solution-related action items. This is the "price we must pay" for creativity and open-mindedness.

12. While waiting for data or statistical analyses, an occasional meeting may be canceled in advance. After several months, schedule the routine meetings half as often.

13. Try to have projects result from control charted variables to ensure that system problems do actually exist. Progress can be monitored as you go out-of-control on the good side of the centerline. This normally shows up as runs on the same side of the center line. Celebrate all lasting improvements. Give the team members certificates for a free pizza. (They already have enough baseball caps with the company logo on them.) Let their families participate in the fun!

14. There will generally be several actions required to solve system problems. The team creates an opportunities list with cost estimates, priorities, timing, and actions needed by upper management, etc. The opportunities are implemented one at a time and progress monitored on the control charts.

15. The operating managers are carefully trained by the team to enable them to learn to respond to local faults and not to hold their local people responsible for system problems. The system problems are delegated to the prevention team.

16. It is likely best not to "fall into the trap" of reporting at routine periodical business meetings about where we are pertaining to the schedule. Most systems problems cannot be solved "against the clock." The "clock" is often a large part of the problem.

17. The team is formed around specific problems (projects) and everything is data-based. Departmentalization and suboptimization will be reduced, and the culture will be improved, but as a spinoff and over the long term. Attempts to date to quickly change cultures so that the new philosophy can "take root" have been mostly ineffective. Cultures change by total immersion in the Deming vision, by example, and over the long term. The teams are ad hoc to solve a specific problem or to take advantage of an opportunity. Cultural changes are a nice side effect.

18. The team leader must have considerable finesse to see that a major objective is to develop the motivation and skills of team members.

19. Team spirit may wane at times, but this must not be for long. Off-hours contact is very important to nurture the team culture and morale. Business breakfasts, barbecues, etc., are a must.

20. Focus on group praise. Top management must be tutored on how to praise teams, versus singling out heroes. All firms have "fast burners" who seem to do no wrong. Management has to individually nurture these egos and keep them in the limelight. It may be best to keep these people off the teams, or at a minimum, counsel them on the team-recognition theme.

21. When problem solving, do it in two phases. First, identify problems, then work out possible solutions.

22. Regardless of their technical expertise, keep the employees with ill dispositions off the teams.

23. The team leader must constantly be on the lookout for "hidden agendas." The research and author's experience support the fact that this is the number one reason for team failure.[11] "Boss watching" is a major creativity-destroying hidden agenda. (Thanks to Dr. Ken Blanchard, of the *One-Minute Manager* fame, for helping me appreciate this fact.)

One of Deming's 14 Points is "to drive out fear." Interdepartmental teams can help do this. The uncertainty of management's knee-jerk responses to common cause variability certainly creates employee anxiety. As the employees see management "owning up" to system problems and reacting appropriately, many of the flustered faces leaving the office at exactly 5 P.M. (set your watch by them!) are replaced by more contented expressions leaving work later because they are constructively helping the firm to continually improve. (Keep reading. The next section may be about you!)

Deeply rooted in many of Deming's writings is what he learned from the Japanese about continual improvement. Over the long haul, small bits of successive improvement (often nonmeasurable, not hero-producing) add up to substantial gains. The interdepartmental team approach is the most successful method to enable firms to continually improve. Will up-front management support make the teams successful? No, not in isolation. The team must be constructed and managed properly. Management support is what Herzberg called a maintenance factor.[12] You must have it to elevate the group to the point of having the capability to achieve. But to convert this capability into action takes skill, with special attention to nurturing the social needs of the group to keep it cohesive.

It takes tremendous skill and nurturing by an insightful leader to lead an interdepartmental team, and I am sure there are many helpful tips that others could add to this chapter. Certainly listening skills are a must, along with diplomacy and common sense. Charisma and public speaking skills are a must also! The author is aware of a large firm whose first team effort failed miserably. The only team recommendation presented to management was an employee "pet" project, consisting of a massive capital expansion project that had been turned down several times before. The team leader should have diplomatically led the problem-solving sessions toward several other smaller, but profitable projects that could (would) be implemented. Then employees would have seen management finally taking action (even in a small way) to improve the system versus, as in the past, simply trying to jawbone them into doing it all for the company (which was impossible) while the bosses did whatever it was they did in the front office. On the other hand, management would have also seen the employees positively helping the firm to continually improve. Communications and morale would have improved, and the culture would have begun to improve. Success builds on success. Future projects would have thus become easier.

Considering the entire firm as "the team" and expecting synergies and interdepartmental solutions to naturally evolve is generally far too optimistic except for the most simple issues. Smaller, effectively managed interdepartmental teams are the modus operandi of the future. In fact, they are a necessity for survival beyond five to 10 years. A plant of 400 employees will likely have three to four teams in existence at any one time. A recent *Fortune* survey revealed that the most innovative firms like 3M, GE, and Kimberly-Clark are masters of the interdepartmental team.[13]

Figure 2.7 is redrawn for convenience. Remember, the firm had experienced no lasting reductions in scrap rate for at least six years prior to point A.

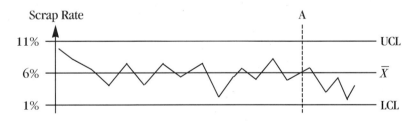

Figure 2.7   Plant Scrap Rate

The interdepartmental team was formed and its recommendations were phased in. There was an interim period of six months (not shown). It took six months for the team to generate its recommendations. The plot to the right of point A shows the new results. The average scrap rate was about one percentage point lower and approaching the theoretical limit, because a certain amount of pattern cut-out scrap is an inherent part of this process. Note that the plus or minus variability was only about one-third its old level. There were no more counterproductive responses to unreasonable management pressure. Since scrap was either finished product that could not be shipped, or raw materials (in-process) that were not used, any lowering of variability enabled a corresponding reduction in inventories. How do you implement just-in-time (JIT) inventory systems? The same way you improve quality or increase productivity. Set up a real-time system to quickly identify local faults (an SPC chart is superb), analyze the statistical nature of the data to establish when mostly system problems are what are left, convene and manage interdepartmental teams, and then follow the team's recommendations. The resulting minimal variability will enable the JIT implementation tools to be subsequently effective.

As you will see later, several of Deming's 14 Points involve statistical training for the masses. One must not be too hasty to spend this decade's training budget without a road map. It should be clearer to you by now why a deep statistical vision is necessary, and only one of the many useful statistical tools has been discussed so far: the SPC chart.

The next section is a primer on problem-solving tools for the interdepartmental teams. First, for enlightenment, what are some typical system problems? Those marked with asterisks existed in the carton plant that had scrap rate opportunities. Anyone could add a dozen more items.

- Poor job descriptions
- Outdated job descriptions*
- Ambient condition problems*
- Poor or insufficient training*

- Lack of statistical vision*
- Wrong or no raw material specs
- Poor product designs
- Inadequate testing of prototypes
- Poor supervision: not communicative, ignorant, etc.*
- Lack of adequate preventive maintenance*
- Fatigue
- Management overcontrol: quality thrust now, production later, back and forth*
- "Ship it anyway" culture
- Inaccessible leaders
- Poor pay and benefits — too much turnover
- Nonstatistical targets and specs*
- Nonstatistically determined budgets*
- Vendor-shopping by the purchasing manager for lowest cost*
- Competing objectives imposed by management*
- An accounting system that rewards only short-term results*
- Increased variability by the knee-jerk response*
- Performance appraisal systems that cause discontent or reduce teamwork
- Promotions often from the outside
- Unmeasurable data not considered
- Ineffective employee selection techniques
- No knowledge of ergonomics
- Product mix not with process capabilities*
- Untrained supervisors
- Wages below community average for skill levels
- Unmaintained equipment
- No unifying corporate mission statement
- Hidden management by objectives (MBO) practitioners
- Grudge-holding managers
- Some managers "asleep at the wheel"
- Unnecessary bureaucratic procedures
- Insufficient funding for preventive maintenance
- Training mostly by on-the-job training (OJT)
- Creative employees stymied by the number crunchers

- An accounting system that punishes preventive thinking
- Poor machine designs
- Multiple vendors
- Sales force not knowledgeable of process capabilities
- A confusing, untrusted accounting system
- Constant management turnover
- Lack of trust of management
- Outdated, confusing business forms
- Purchasing employees unaware of operational needs
- No useful raw material specs (operational definitions)
- Uncooperative company-owned vendors
- Uncoordinated JIT
- No standard operating procedures (SOPs)
- Outdated SOPs
- Inoperative tools and gages
- Machines pushed beyond design capabilities
- Engineering and technical staff too lean
- Customers' needs not known
- Employees unaware of internal customers' needs
- Variable machine setup times
- Poor standardization of machine parts
- Inadequate office telephone system
- No privacy for transacting sensitive business
- All expenditures subjected to return on investment (ROI), net present value (NPV), or payback targets
- Customer feedback not categorized, or not representative
- Political clout required to get maintenance performed
- Harried managers only responding to "squeaking wheels"

The next section pertains to problem-solving tools often used by interdepartmental teams. Remember, the interdepartmental teams generally serve to identify and eliminate common causes (system problems) like the ones just listed. The local employees can usually rid the job of the local faults, especially when they have statistics to help spotlight them, SPC and Pareto charts, for example. After things are put into a state of statistical control, unless management then initiates interdepartmental teams of some sort to reduce the common causes, the situation will eventually regress back to its old state.

Managers generally give more than enough attention to the absolute value of things such as production quantity, sales, measurable quality aspects, safety, costs, inventories, etc. If an equal amount of attention were paid to reducing variability, the business world would operate considerably more effectively and efficiently. Variability is the root of most problems facing businesses today. The knee-jerk response resulting from treating common causes as local faults is *the* major contributing problem behind the reduced competitiveness of the United States. You often hear, "The harder we try the worse it gets!" Some more creative approaches for solving problems are discussed in the next section.

Problem Solving
Obstacles

This section contains some tools that can aid in problem solving. It is somewhat technical and could almost be relegated to an appendix. Do not get bored and put the book down; the visionary stuff comes later. During later sections of the book when the interdepartmental team concept is discussed, it is important that you already know how the groups operate. You will find other lists in the literature with considerably more tools, some of which are okay. The ones in this section have been found by the author to be most useful. It may be best not to inundate your teams with too many techniques beyond the ones listed here. In many cases it first seems that these ideas are more conceptual models for organizing one's thoughts, than distinct tools such as a ruler or a calculator. There are management teams that solve complex problems effectively with seemingly no use of these tools. However, as one investigates their thought processes, it becomes apparent that many of these problem-solving tools are being used informally, or under different names. In contrast, some teams have superb SPC and problem-solving training and could teach seminars in these techniques; however, very few long-term chronic problems are getting solved because they do not understand and practice the Deming vision. In these cases the day-to-day fires may be extinguished, but there is no vision about how to prevent the emergencies prior to the crisis state. Without a deep understanding and use of the statistical Deming vision, the firm will likely never get beyond the "fire fighting" stage. The resulting demoralization and employee burnout leads to apathy, or worse, so much turnover that new hires are having to ineffectively deal with complex issues they are not ready for yet. There are many obvious reasons behind this lack of vision, such as personality issues, not enough technical staff, etc. However, two not so obvious, but important reasons for team failures emerge and will be discussed here. (Let the big boss read this page!)

The first is the "hero syndrome." In most firms, the only way to get noticed among the "struggling crowd" is to single-handedly solve big problems and have this come to the attention of management (be John Wayne, not Henry Fonda). In other words, management has not learned how to promote and reward teamwork, and this in turn has created barriers between departments. This behavior was probably acceptable during the formative years of the firm when there were so many big problems that a person could likely score big on a frequent basis, solving problems that seemed almost tailor made to their specialized talents. However, with the exception of a few of the Silicon Valley type firms, most companies have matured technically beyond the days when the problems were so narrow and obvious that sole individuals could make many lasting, significant system changes. Most problems today are interdepartmental and require a team approach. The issues today are also seldom short-term, but require many months of investigative and implementation effort. There will be many examples of typical interdepartmental problems in later chapters.

Upper management must realize this phenomenon and literally force employees to form interdepartmental prevention teams to solve chronic problems, one at a time. Considerable training and nurturing will be required by the employees.

The second reason for a lack of vision pertaining to long-term problem prevention relates to upper management's control by the numbers with no SPC charts, as discussed in the previous sections. Many more examples of this will follow.

Upper management must organize and train the people to use the concept of the interdepartmental team. Even more importantly, the local employees cannot be held responsible for a troublesome financial or administrative variable that is mostly in-statistical-control, hence no local faults. If the employees are pressured to "do something" when only random deviations away from the average exist, ineffective knee-jerk reactions result initially. Eventually, frustration, burnout, and lack of vision (energy) will result. As management stresses quality today, production tomorrow, and waste the next day, etc., the latest issue gets a bandage at the expense of the others. This causes tremendous system variability that makes the problem even worse. For all front office variables used to evaluate or motivate people, there should be a control chart, or else forget the numbers and use intuition! (Many examples are included in a later section.) Upper management must also be able to distinguish system problems from local faults, and to lead the employees through the interdepartmental team approach for system problems. Each interdepartmental team should be formed to work on a specific control charted variable or group of system issues. Most firms can only handle one or two teams at a specific location in the beginning, perhaps five or six after a year. The initial projects must be chosen carefully to ensure initial successes that can be subsequently flaunted.

With the elimination of the Deadly Diseases and the proper execution of interdepartmental teams, be prepared to capitalize on your new found level of creativity, energy, and teamwork. Challenge the employees with new levels of expected excellence to keep complacency from setting in. Now to several problem-solving tools. See Gitlow, Ishikawa, and Scherkenbach for further details on problem solving.

Brainstorming

Under the leadership of a team coach who can tolerate the ambiguity and who has the charisma to get people to talk freely, brainstorming is a technique used to generate a creative list of issues, problems, and/or solutions. Under typical daily pressures to keep quiet and not look stupid, many creative ideas do not surface. Brainstorming can break this barrier at times.

The rules of brainstorming are as follows:

1. The problem or issue is explained and then each team member is asked to create a list of every item that comes to mind. "Freewheeling" is emphasized. The coach explains to them that everyone will probably have a few wild ideas. They are asked not to critique or evaluate their ideas, just "go with the flow."
2. The coach writes on a big board as each member shares an idea. Members can pass if their list is exhausted. The coach warns that no items are evaluated at this point.
3. The process is repeated until all idea lists are exhausted.
4. The next step is to openly evaluate the list. Some ideas can be combined or deleted.

The list can be incorporated onto a fishbone chart (discussed in the next section) or left in tabular form. The next step is to prioritize the list based on group consensus. This prioritization can take several forms depending on the number of items. In any event the coach is going to summarize the votes in a matrix format during a session. Each team member may be assigned a certain number of points to be distributed among the items based on his or her perception of the priorities. Then by combining people's votes in the summary matrix, drastically different team members can be given a chance to explain their nonconformance. A new vote can be taken if the nonconformists seem to have a point. Eventually, one to three action items usually emerge as top priorities. For system problems, you will find that upper management help becomes a must at this time. As the team is progressing to this point, the leader must be talking to the relevant upper managers to get a feel for budgetary constraints and company priorities. These considerations must be incorporated into the prioritization scheme (not brainstorming) because it is a must that the list presented to management be implemented, starting *now*. Everyone expects upper management to get defensive, but they usually do not. It is like a "breath of fresh air" for most of them to get candid, implementable recommendations. When this technique works, it can be "magic." It is usually best not to try to do this all during one session. Contemplate a bit!

Fishbone (Cause and Effect) Charts

Analyze the fishbone chart in Figure 2.8 for a moment.

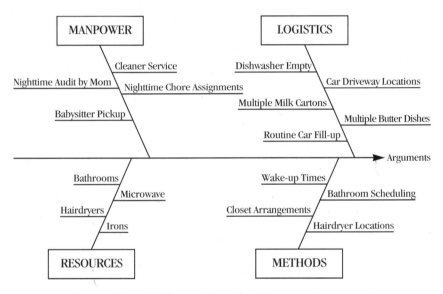

Figure 2.8   Fishbone Chart for Morning Arguments

As a simple example, assume that a family wants to discontinue having arguments in the morning. Through brainstorming the family counselor summarizes their comments on the chart. There is no magic to the chart; it is merely for demonstration purposes. It can, however, make a multifaceted problem seem clearer. Many times in business meetings the group gets into too much detail too quickly. A fishbone chart can help here. The coach can make an emphatic statement that on the first day, only the major categories (see the boxes) will be identified. Then on later days, each major category will be taken one at a time and discussed thoroughly.

Control Charts

The most powerful problem-solving tool is the control chart. A major issue is whether the team is facing a long-term system problem (hence, in-statistical-control, but bad), or local faults manifested by plotted points out-of-statistical-control. A record-keeping system must be set up so that when a local fault occurs, the assignable cause can be identified and eliminated. Something extraordinary usually leads to local faults. All teams should revolve around data and control charts, especially for the first several endeavors. Management wants to measure results, and this is okay as long as it is over the long term and with statistical validity. See Fellers for a complete discussion of the mathematics of control charts.

The problems existing when the charts are in-control are usually systemic and will require a detailed team approach. Expect the resolution of system problems to take months or years.

Pareto Charts

In the early part of this century, Pareto stated that 80 percent of the problems in the world are caused by 20 percent of the people. Pertaining to sociological or manufacturing issues, these odds seem to prevail quite often. (I think God is trying to simplify the world for us, if we will just pay attention statistically.) It is very common for 20 percent of the defect conditions to account for 80 percent of the costs of poor quality or 80 percent of your vendor problems come from 20 percent of the suppliers. A Pareto chart similar to Figure 2.9 can help managers identify the vital few issues.

In this example, 80 percent of the customer returns were shipped on the last 20 percent of the days of the month. Obviously, the plant management had a monthly quota to meet so they did anything to get it out the door on time. This was a real example! Can you believe it? This company, however, no longer exists. They expended so much energy meeting quotas and managing by-the-numbers with no statistical vision, that the harried, burned-out executives failed to see that their only product was going to be nonexistent within a few years.

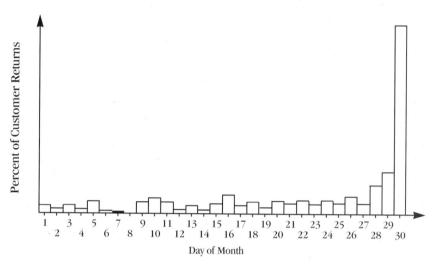

Figure 2.9   *Pareto Chart of Customer Returns Versus Shipment Date*

Pareto charts are a must for presenting data to management. It is at times useful to consider double classifications. For example, day shipped and production foreman, as a double classification scheme, may show that some individuals need more help than others.

Trend Charts

A trend chart is a control chart with no control limits. These are particularly useful when only the long-run trend is of interest, or when the average is constantly changing, making a control chart ineffective. Figure 2.10 contains a trend chart for scrap rate resulting from the dismantling of an MBO system centering around daily production quotas. With the process average consistently changing as in Figure 2.10, it would be impossible to establish SPC limits until things stabilize a bit.

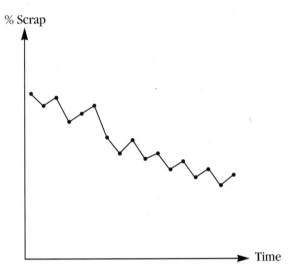

Figure 2.10   Trend Chart for Scrap Rate

Scatter Diagrams

There are many correlated variables in a manufacturing plant. However, common cause (random) variability often makes it difficult to visualize these correlations without a scatter diagram, as shown in Figure 2.11.

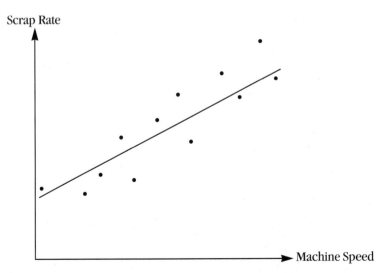

Figure 2.11   Scatter Diagram for Machine Speed Versus Scrap

Experimental Design (Factorial Experiments)

A major technical reason making it difficult for business people to solve problems is the misunderstood concept of interaction among variables. Interaction is the situation where the effect of one variable is a function of the level of another variable. This concept is demonstrated graphically in Figure 2.12.

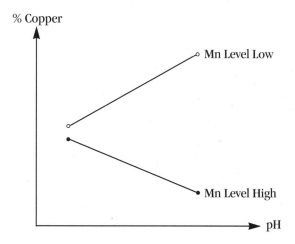

Figure 2.12   Interaction Among Variables

In this case, the percent copper in a brass plating seemed uncontrollable. Upon further analysis, it was discovered that the effect of plating-bath pH could not be identified in isolation. By subplotting incoming steel rod from the vendors into high and low manganese levels and then running trials with different pH values, the managers were able to see that as the manganese levels varied, the effect of pH changes varied. In this particular case, all interesting levels of each variable were studied at all interesting levels of all other variables. This is called a factorial experiment. Factorial experiments are beyond the scope of this text, but are one of the few methods of identifying inter-action. Interaction can be suspected when the following are true:

1. Every day seems different.
2. Problems come and go before you can identify the causes.

3. Problems seem different during some seasons of the year.
4. Problems often coincide with raw material batch or vendor changes, but not always.
5. Experiments have not been conducted across departmental boundaries.
6. Departments have competing numerical objectives.

When the author is asked to participate in the resolution of a specific, long-term problem in a manufacturing plant, he always initially suspects that there are some troublesome, unknown interactions in effect. Engineers are typically schooled to consider the effects of variables one at a time. This approach makes it extremely difficult to identify many elusive problems. All practicing engineers need to be schooled by a master pertaining to the multivariate, interactive nature of the physical world.

This next comment will probably not make it past the reviewers of this book who may teach experimental design workshops, but here it is! The internal people are not likely to be able to "go it alone" in applying experimental design without the hands-on guidance of a master statistician. Attendance at a two or three week seminar as a sole strategy never seems to reach the bottom line pertaining to quality or productivity improvements. Some visionary training for the insiders is required, however. Try to do it in-house; two or three days may suffice if the master teacher stays with you to help make it work.

Regression Analysis

We have been discussing factorial designs that are typically used to help establish what the major causative variables of a process are and what the most desirable levels of the variables seem to be. The next level of knowledge that one likely wants is the equation relating the product response variable and the input process variables. As shown below, Y is the output process response variable and the X's are the input process variables:

$$Y = B_0X_0 + B_1X_1 + B_2X_2 + \ldots + B_7X_7$$

If one is extremely careful, regression analysis sometimes can be used to find the best-fit functional relationship and to establish how much of the variability in Y can be attributed to the various process X variables. This typically, however, involves the use of an experienced statistician and a large amount of data. Two or three levels of each variable (X) will not yield a reliable solution unless the relationship is very linear and well defined over the range of interest. A problem with regression analysis and computers is that the "best-fit" equation is always provided, even when this best-fit is not a good fit. The computer only finds the coefficients for the functional form specified. If the true functional form has squared terms or interproduct terms $(X_I X_J)$, $I \neq J$, resulting from I/J interactions, unless we know how to specify the functional form, we will get an incorrect linear functional form (by default or intentionally). An experienced statistics practitioner can sometimes spot problems like these, however.

Many engineers have tried using regression analysis and become frustrated with the obviously wrong answers, such as negative coefficients that are known to be positive. See Fellers for a more complete discussion of the pitfalls and idiosyncracies of regression analysis. There are no intuitive reasons behind some of these idiosyncrasies of regression analysis. Often, however, an experienced statistician can "get around" these problems. Do not be completely discouraged; regression analysis can provide answers to processing issues, but extreme caution is warranted.

In many processing-type industries, controlled factorial experiments (experimental design) cannot be run, for a multitude of reasons. In these cases, regression analysis of historical data can often provide some answers pertaining to the vital few variables.

Flowcharts

In some cases flowcharts like the one shown in Figure 2.13 can be used during team meetings to clarify confusing process issues.

Many experienced interdepartmental team coaches say that they never delve too deeply into any problem without first flowcharting it. The author, however, has not found them to be necessary for all occasions.

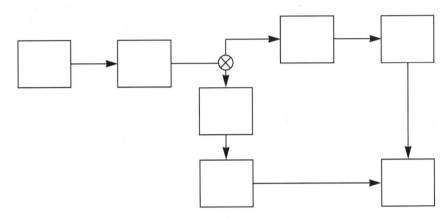

Figure 2.13   Flowchart

Concluding Remarks on Problem Solving

Many interdepartmental teams force the discipline of rational problem solving by requiring that all of the above tools be completed. This is usually not a requirement, but can work. It is never recommended to eliminate brainstorming, however. It is typically obvious what the problem-solving process should be for the team. The important concept is the discipline of forcing the team approach and rewarding team success.

The author has seen many chronic problems solved through the interdepartmental approach. Some of these problems were in existence for many years as hero-hopefuls tried numerous short-term, bandage solutions. The team approach is slow, but eventually successful. The big challenge is for management to encourage team behavior versus the hero syndrome, and to show highly visible support and patience.

H. G. Wells once stated that the day will come when a knowledge of statistics will be almost a requirement for citizenship. Deming has explained that experience can only be catalogued and put to use rationally by the application of statistical theory and that if you rely solely on experience, things will never get better. Perhaps you can begin to understand the validity of their comments.

More Examples

To compete in today's international markets, most businesses are trying desperately to reduce inventories. As in the quality movement in the United States beginning in 1980, the Japanese also "brought us to our knees" pertaining to inventories. Their space limitations, smallness mentality, and cultural trait of thriftiness by necessity gave the Japanese an incentive to learn to operate with little or no inventories. This fact, along with a typical inventory holding cost of 35 cents on the dollar per year, has certainly put most business persons on alert. Why do we hold inventories? To compensate for system variabilities such as varying quality, uncertain lead times, changing processing times, forecast accuracies, etc. Obviously, things do vary, but at times we make it worse because of no statistical vision. Once again, if we cannot statistically distinguish local faults from common cause, we may fail to approach the problem correctly or may elicit an unwanted response that unnecessarily increases variability. In the next several examples, see how the Deming vision applies. All examples are actual cases, unless stated otherwise.

In a large manufacturing firm, the corporate accountant decided that for a very expensive constituent part of their product, the usage variance must be reduced. The typical plant was absorbing approximately $70,000 too much of this material per month, as it seemed. A young eager man on the corporate staff explained to the financial vice president that this was a waste of over $7 million per year across all facilities. "Something must be done," he said. Little did they know that the pressure on the manufacturing folks, with the corporate technocrats possessing little processing knowledge and no statistical vision, was going to cause things to get worse. It was decided that all unfavorable monthly variances exceeding $50,000 required a report to corporate management explaining what was wrong and how the problem was (or would be) corrected. After this directive, morale became terrible, junior plant accountants began looking for new jobs, and the inventory variance actually got worse. What they did not do at corporate was to analyze the control chart of several years' data as shown in Figure 2.14. (See Fellers for a discussion of control charts

Figure 2.14   Inventory Variance In-Control

for individual numbers such as the one shown here.)

This SPC chart was constructed later by an interdepartmental team and was from data before the new policy began. The people at corporate headquarters did not know to construct the plot in advance or how to analyze such data. With statistical vision, one could have seen that this process was in-statistical-control. Consequently, the local people would not likely be able to have any lasting impact on the problem. What was needed was some sort of upper management action resulting from recommendations of an interdepartmental team.

The first half of the next chart in Figure 2.15 contains the data of the previous figure from before the new corporate decision came down to the plants. The second half of the plot in Figure 2.15 resulted when the new, nonvisionary policy went into effect. As you can see, things got worse.

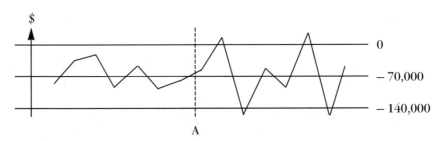

Figure 2.15   Things Got Worse — Knee-Jerk Response

The new directive required action when there was an unfavorable variance exceeding $50,000; however, just from the natural capabilities of the system and common cause, by chance it was almost always worse than this threshold (spec). It did not matter what the financial vice president wanted to happen, the local plant people could not make lasting system improvements. There were no local faults. However, they tried. Starting at point A in Figure 2.15, notice that their efforts made it worse. One week there was pressure to use less of this material, and the production operators did so. Then the quality inspectors would start finding finished product items that failed usage tests because of an insufficient amount of this material. Then there was pressure by the local management to improve quality by using more material, back and forth, ad infinitum. The knee-jerk response had begun. You can see the increase in variability to the right of point A in Figure 2.15. Note that the average unfavorable variance got even worse, and costs went up. To try to remedy this situation, some of the plant accountants began making up lies to tell the corporate accountants. This was in an attempt to enable the production people to attenuate the knee-jerk response forced on the local operators. This is called "survival lying." The anxiety within the plant accountants by being forced to lie in order to do their jobs led many of them to seek new employment. Some left, and new hires came in and started the knee-jerk response again. This type of stress and the resulting effect on the health of employees is a killer! Will the corporate technocrats have to answer for this on Judgment Day? Probably not. How could they have known? Upper management must train, enlighten, and make sure that statistical vision is incorporated into every decision. No exceptions!

The end of this story was a happy one. The author convinced the corporate staff to create an interdepartmental team. There were a number of system problems that were solved. The largest contributing problem enlightened us to one of Deming's 14 Points (sole sourcing). The purchasing people, by upper management directive, were buying this raw material from 12 sources, all of which were acceptable, but different. They were bargain shopping with little knowledge of the impact and true cost of this practice. Also, the engineers at corporate staff established the material usage standard from one package of product from a single, exceptionally good vendor. When the varying material (from differing vendors) was loaded onto the machine in the factory, the operators had no way of knowing which vendor supplied it. To compensate for this vendor-to-vendor variability, the operators on the average used too much material to compensate for the seemingly random low density rolls of raw material. After the interdepartmental team finished its job, the best, most consistent two vendors were chosen, and near sole sourcing thus began. We had started the Deming transition. The sole vendors and this firm became partners. Their technical transactions, versus the old adversarial arms-length relationship, saved both sides millions of dollars. And by the way, the purchase price came down, not to mention the reduced administrative cost of fewer vendors and increased operational efficiencies in the plants. It took about a year to get a solution from the interdepartmental team and to implement it. The net result was an inventory variance variable centered about zero (as you would expect) with common cause of plus or minus about $30,000 per month. In the end, the accountant's threshold or action limit of $50,000 seemed reasonable. In fact, it was changed to plus or minus $30,000. There was also a considerable saving in inventory holding costs. With half the variability in usage, only half the level of material inventory safety stock was needed. One can begin to see why it is so difficult to sell to most Japanese manufacturers. They have their vendor partners, like in this example, and are unwilling to bargain shop or to break with these proven suppliers. They work as a team in the "extended process."

A note of caution pertaining to the last example. It is unlikely that you will see such a case; however, it could have been that the average unfavorable inventory variance was initially an average of minus $70,000 because of sloppiness and a simple lack of managerial pressure to pay attention. In an unusual case like this, simple managerial pressure may provide a lasting solution because the system problem has been solved; poor supervision has been improved. If simple poor supervision was not the total system problem, but was treated as such, which is frequently the case, watch things closely after managerial pressure is intensified. Something else in the organization will deteriorate as a "relief valve" since no real needed system adjustments were made. Typical relief valves are:

- Quality goes down.
- Customer complaints go up.
- Fatigue diminishes the creative spirit.
- Preventive maintenance is shorted.
- Production goes down.
- Employee turnover goes up.
- Safety suffers.
- A union drive is started.
- There are fewer smiling faces entering the facility in the morning.

Some of these types of relief-valve problems can be subtle (but devastating) and are generally always delayed responses. At times it is not clear for months who was at fault. By this time because of typical short-term reward systems, it may have no effect on the culprit's evaluations, pay, or future career. Management must learn to prevent such occurrences.

In a case of simple lack of supervision, it would have been most effective to let the interdepartmental team recommend more management pressure, assuming it was warranted, before "jumping the gun" and blaming hourly employees again. If the typical manager could spend several days at the lowest levels, in the trenches, as a "fly on the wall" with no protectionary behavior by the employees (as the author has many times), he or she would learn more than what comes out of 10 years worth of data from management feedback systems such as cost accounting reports, production summaries, budget deviations, etc.

The next example was provided by a student as a response to a test question. The question stated: "Tell me of a case when you were personally harmed because the boss did not have the statistical vision."

As stated by the student: "My first job was at a large chain grocery store. Management was divided into upper and lower areas.

Lower management was more aware of certain problems than upper management. For instance, we unloaded supply trucks once a week and it was understood that some merchandise would fall off of the conveyer belt. We would recognize that three to four boxes of 'something' would fall off and break. Lower management understood this and didn't worry about the situation. One day the general manager walked in when a case of 'something' fell off of the belt. He almost had a stroke, and he couldn't wait to jump on me. He told me how sloppy we were and that we *had* to do better. The box that broke was probably the second box to fall off the conveyer the entire day. We were well 'within the system.' "

A person statistically trained to create control charts could show that if the system average was four broken boxes per day, the upper control limit was probably 10 boxes. So an average of four boxes fell every time, and occasionally nine or 10 boxes would be broken as an isolated occurrence with the system still in-control. This meant that only management could improve the situation in a lasting fashion if this number of broken boxes was unacceptable. The following are some likely system problems:

- Too much pressure to finish quickly.
- Conveyor moving too fast.
- Poor instructions or training.
- Poor supervision gives employees the jitters.

Another example is from a college student, powerless to strike back because he had to work to pay tuition expenses. It is no surprise that morale is often low and unions represent some employees.

"I worked as a driver for a large pizza chain in 1986. The manager had never delivered a pizza and had no idea what it took to deliver a pizza. I had delivered for other stores before going to work for this pizza place. From experience I found that there were several steps that a driver must go through when delivering an order. These were:

1. Finding the address on an area map.
2. Preparing drinks and other items ordered with the pizza. (Sometimes 1 and 2 could be done while the pizza is still in the oven.)
3. Putting the pizza in a hot bag and the drinks in a drink rack.
4. Loading the pizza and drinks in the car.
5. Pulling out of the parking lot. (This is not always easy when the store is located on a busy road.)
6. Locating the house.
7. Unloading the pizza and drinks and walking them up to the customer's door.
8. Waiting for someone to answer the door.
9. Exchanging money for the pizza. (This takes a while if the person is paying with a check.)
10. Walking back to the car, driving back to the store, unloading the hot bag and drink rack and walking back up to the store.

"On a good delivery, this took 20 to 35 minutes. The average time was 27 minutes.

The store manager and area manager 'once' drove from the store to different locations in the delivery area around the store. They found that it takes 20 minutes or less to drive from the store to an address and back. The managers did not take most of the above steps into account. They also refused to listen when the drivers tried to explain why all runs could not be made in 20 minutes. Drivers were reprimanded when runs were not completed in 20 minutes."

The boss on "one" occasion possibly under minimally adverse traffic, established that he could make any run in 20 minutes. NO STATISTICAL VISION! How do you do this type thing accurately, if at all? Make 30 or more trips with several drivers across every day of the week. Then it would be clear, as the employee stated, that the system average was 27 minutes, and the control limits were plus or minus seven minutes.

An example from Deming now follows. In a welding operation,

the average number of faults per 5,000 welds was 9.55 occurrences. In statistical jargon:

$$\bar{c} = 9.55$$
$$\text{UCL} = \bar{c} + 3\sqrt{\bar{c}} = 19$$
$$\text{LCL} = \bar{c} - 3\sqrt{\bar{c}} = 0$$

If a chronological plot of many periodic 5,000 unit samples shows the system to be in-control, and if a bad weld is dangerous, keep your liability insurance premiums paid up. A system problem(s) exists requiring a lengthy interdepartmental team investigation. Badgering the employees to do better is useless, demoralizing, and typically cost increasing. If the system is definitely in-control, it does little good "to rub an employee's nose" in an identified bad weld. The same system that produced the bad ones also produced the good ones. What were the likely system problems? Who knows? Probably only an interdepartmental team!

A typical control chart that is often recommended for defect situations like the previous example is a c-chart. As an example, a consumer products firm purchased corrugated containers from several vendors, all of which were equally good. One of them, however, occasionally had an annoying defect of no bar code on isolated boxes. The occurrence rate was extremely low, so it was like "a needle in a haystack" in the vendor's plant to sort them out. Hence, no fractional sampling plan would be useful, and 100 percent testing was completely infeasible. (Not to mention usually ineffective in the general case.) The purchasing firm was near sole sourcing, three vendors instead of the previous nine, and had formed technical partnerships with each vendor. Hence, there was no adversarial arm's-length relationship. Consequently, they could work as a customer-vendor team. It occurred to the vendor that since the customer, in effect, inspects all of their units, perhaps some SPC at the receiving plant could help them establish the basic nature of their problem. Was it local faults and thus sloppy work habits, or was it a system problem in which their local workers were probably

Missing Bar Codes

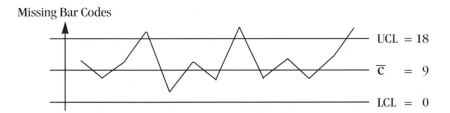

UCL = 18

$\overline{c}$ = 9

LCL = 0

Figure 2.16   Weekly Number of Missing Bar Codes

doing their best? (It was decided that the summary interval would be weekly for statistical reasons. A c-chart, as shown in Figure 2.16, is typically used things are counted, versus measured. See Fellers for a more complete discussion of c-charts.) The control chart is shown in Figure 2.16.

There were recurring weeks when the process was out-of-control, indicating the presence of local faults that must be eliminated to stabilize the system. During a local analysis, the employees found that these were the weeks that a certain operator happened to start a new run and was prone to not placing the printing dies properly. The after-the-fact SPC chart showed this. Following the normal rules of SPC, the system average of nine was previously established not including the out-of-control points. Consequently, with nine occurrences per week common to the system, there was also a background system problem, but the local faults had to be removed first. It is very difficult to improve the system when it is unstable. You never know whether you are looking at system noise (common cause) or an immediate change (a local fault). The major system problem here was no formal die retirement plan after a certain number of impressions. The operators had been told to get as many impressions as they can, with no bad printing. This is like my wife telling me to speed up, but I better not get a ticket — and I am already going 62 mph in a 55 mph zone! The interdepartmental team did a mean time between failure (MTBF) study to establish a die change-out recipe that by design gave no bad printing. The problem was solved forever! The cost? Almost zero. Everybody was happy, except one young engineer who was convinced that they needed another gadget to sort out the defective boxes.

Teaching Goodness

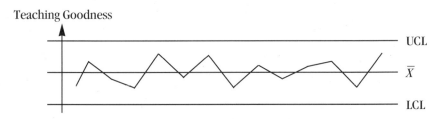

Figure 2.17   Daily Measure of
Teaching Performance for One Professor

Now, a more philosophical example follows in which there are no data from which anyone could construct a control chart, but the Deming vision could help a group of administrators decide not to make a potentially demoralizing decision. At a particular first-class southern college, there was pressure on the administration to give more rewards for good teaching versus sole attention to research performance, or worse, the "squeaking wheel." Obviously, this was an admirable desire by the faculty and administration. Before critiquing a proposed teaching evaluation procedure, consider the conceptual control chart in Figure 2.17.

Who knows how to quantify teaching goodness, except maybe the students five to 10 years later, and who has asked them lately? In any event, it should be clear from Figure 2.17 that from day-to-day, all faculty will randomly vary about their average ($\overline{X}$). No one can be their best every day. To think otherwise simply does not make sense! Of course, we all want teachers with a good average and low variability about that average, as manifested by the difference between UCL and LCL. Now to the procedure proposed to the college administrators.

It was suggested by a committee (not a properly run interdepartmental team) that each quarter, one faculty member be secretly appointed to randomly audit one other teacher. Then a measure of observed teaching goodness was to be provided to the administration. Not to mention rater bias, or the teacher altering the lesson plan because of the auditor, can you see how this recommendation lacked statistical vision and compassion? If a faculty member's rater randomly audits his or her class on a below average day (from common cause), the boss may get the wrong impression. There are methods, based on work sampling to enable one to attempt to do this type of thing; however, the sample size (number of audits) for this situation would be so large that the auditor would probably have to attend almost all the classes to get an accurate assessment of the professor's skill. This would have been completely infeasible, despite the fact that many of us should be taught by some master teachers from time to time! Consider the additional example that follows.

Someone once said that statistical visions and SPC charts do not apply to pure service firms, like banks for example. This statement was very wrong. Consider an example of a corporate bank administrator who was concerned about a particular branch that seemed to be losing too many accounts. Data from 25 quarters for lost accounts per 100 customers across all branches were presented statistically in a control chart. The average for the corporation as a whole ($\overline{c}$) was 2.0; the UCL was 4 and the LCL was 0. (The chart is not shown.) The branch bank in question was frequently outside the company UCL of 4.0 lost accounts per 100 customers; consequently, they were out-of-control. A local fault, or faults, existed in the corporation as a whole, and that branch was the local fault. Now what should be done? A new branch manager was brought in, but nothing changed. Internal to that bank, there were probably some elusive system problems. A control chart just for that branch was finally constructed and is shown in Figure 2.18.

Customer Loss per 100

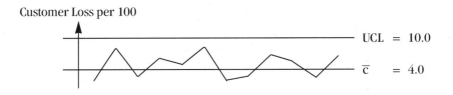

$$\text{UCL} = 10.0$$
$$\overline{c} = 4.0$$

Figure 2.18   Branch Bank In-Control — Bad Average

The statistical vision was now complete. No internal local faults existed for the problem bank; it was not likely that simply trying harder would provide lasting improvements. The subsequent interdepartmental team established that the competition was too extreme in this suburb. The branch should never have been located there. (Hence an upper management mistake!) Another problem was demographic. There were many retirees there who had the time and were quick to comparison shop and then change banks for the biggest toaster. No action was warranted, except lowering the expectations for this bank branch. It cannot meet the objectives of the average bank branch. It cannot meet the objectives of the average bank because of the demographic system problems. At least the employees would not be harried and demoralized. Their improved attitude may increase business. Now to a new example.

The people on Wall Street and in Washington, D.C., create many of our problems in the United States not on purpose, but out of ignorance. The press makes the issue worse! Consider the morning news:

This Month's Trade Deficit Up $1.2 Billion!

Bad news? Suppose so; however, not worthy of reporting or of quickly making a reaction. Consider the control chart in Figure 2.19 for the trade deficit during the period of January 1988 through December 1989.

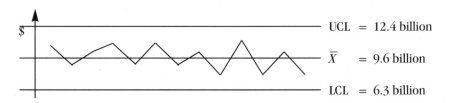

Figure 2.19   Trade Deficit In-Control, but Bad

The latest rise of $1.2 billion was likely a common cause (random) occurrence. Since the trade deficit is in-statistical-control, there are no local faults (issues) that can be quickly addressed. There are, however, many system problems. The bureaucratic drag or the wisdom of our leaders likely prevents the "knee-jerk" response. But why do we have to hear about every random deviation in the media? Just give us the sports scores and Dear Abby! That's enough. If something goes out-of-statistical-control, now that's news!

Quite frequently, variability breeds more instability when the observer is unstatistically trained. Consider the case where a clerk must reconcile the actual inventory on hand with the computer print-out balance. There is a discrepancy between the physical count and the computer figure, the latter is adjusted to equal to the physical count. If the physical count is always perfect, this procedure is acceptable. However, this is seldom the case. The physical count can have as much error as the balance shown by the computer. Consider Figure 2.20 showing a control chart for the computer printout figure minus the physical count.

Note that on the average, the records are off by five units with a

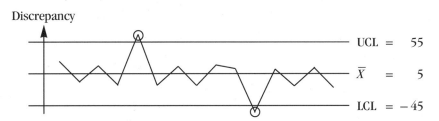

Figure 2.20   *Inventory Discrepancy In-Control*

common cause variability of plus or minus 50. On those two occasions where local faults existed, immediate action was warranted. The clerk or the computer needed some immediate attention. In all the other cases only common causes were present; no local action was warranted, not even an adjustment of the computer figure. This would be a knee-jerk response. (Like a dog chasing its tail, variability from unnecessarily chasing variability!) Upon realizing their mistake of constantly treating system causes as local faults, the firm quit this practice of adjusting the computer balance and the system was allowed to stabilize. The new, and true, limits for common cause were plus or minus 30 instead of 50. Now an interdepartmental team could go to work to reduce the common cause variability. Doing less gave them more stability. Similar situations are everywhere. In this country we expend a considerable amount of resources to make matters even more variable (worse), not to mention the morale, burnout, and stress factor. Back to this inventory example, in the future, unless the discrepancy is out-of-statistical-control, do nothing in the short term. If the average or control limits are intolerable, create an interdepartmental team. When a local fault does occur, take immediate action, because there is a problem. As a result of this new modus operandi, you will eventually gain more credibility. This is in contrast to the old days when you were often guilty of overcontrol and people had grown "numb" to your suggestions!

It is sometimes difficult for perfectionistic, impulsive people to supervise clerical, repetitive operations such as typing or accounts receivables processing. This is especially true when there's no one to help the manager to decipher local faults from system problems and to help him or her to run an interdepartmental team, if necessary. Consider the control chart in Figure 2.21 pertaining to the average, per person, daily typing errors in the secretarial pool. (This was a temporary chart to help analyze the problem. It would not be recommended to keep a watchdog chart like this one for real-time control.)

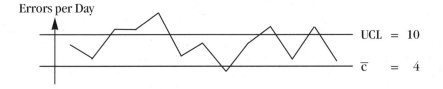

**Figure 2.21   One Person Plotted
on Departmental Chart**

When the secretaries' daily errors were plotted separately on the chart, all of them, except one secretary, were in-statistical-control about the departmental average. This secretary's plot is shown in Figure 2.21. For the larger group of in-control secretaries, whose plots are not shown, there were no local faults. Consequently any improvement for them had to come through the system. An interdepartmental team found that the high-side upper control limit was not tolerable. The major system problem for the in-control secretaries was the disruptive telephone calls and the copy machine gossip. The copier was put in another room. The managers now answer their own phones or receive a private recording through an automated phone system. There was a cost, as well as an immediate payback. The increased efficiency enabled one secretary to be relocated to another job.

Now for the one secretary who was having problems. The individual performance plot on the departmental chart in Figure 2.21 clearly shows this secretary to be having problems. The immediate question pertains to the nature of the problem. Is it insufficient or poor training, lack of capability, or a behavioral problem? To get to the root of the problem, consider the control chart in Figure 2.22 that was constructed using only the data from this secretary, versus the departmental numbers.

Errors per Day

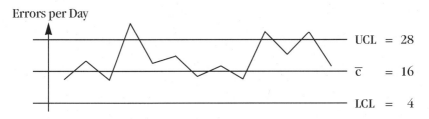

UCL = 28

$\overline{c}$ = 16

LCL = 4

Figure 2.22 Problem Secretary's Chart

Note that the secretary is out-of-control on the individual chart. There are local faults. Perhaps inconsistent work habits was the issue. This was easy to observe and was not the issue. It was eventually found to be lack of training, and in this case, it was not the secretary's fault. Typing errors here were the "tip of the iceberg." On bad days when many errors were made, the secretary was usually flustered because of problems dealing with some other clerical duties that were not well understood. Upon further analysis, the interdepartmental team found that for reasons unknown, this secretary received only OJT, and "sort of" apprenticed with an old, crabby secretary who hated to answer questions and would blow cigarette smoke into her face. OJT as a sole training method is, for most jobs, one of the largest failings of U.S. firms. Professional training is *the* most important issue in a firm.

As a further related example, consider Figure 2.23 for a hypothetical secretary who was trained properly, but whose error rate was high.

Error Rate

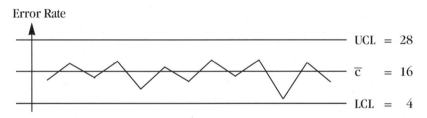

Figure 2.23   In-Control, Unacceptable Secretary

Since the secretary is in-control, there likely will be no local faults, thus no identifiable assignable cause. In this case, according to Deming, additional training of a similar type as given before will be useless. The secretary has stabilized, but probably will never be a good typist. This situation is similar to a new golfer whose handicap stabilizes, but who shoots around 130. This person will never be a golfer. A good way to know when someone is fully trained with the present educational tools is to maintain a control chart to establish when a state of statistical control has been reached. (Four to five consecutive groups of 25 plotted points with one or fewer out-of-control points in each group of 25 indicates a state of control.) After a state of control is achieved, an additional amount of the same type of training would be useless. Another type of training may help, however.

Another example should be informative.[14] Many employees in the firm were complaining about the amount of time it took to process invoices. Vendors were complaining to their internal contacts. The control chart for time to process a purchase order is shown in Figure 2.24.

Time to Process

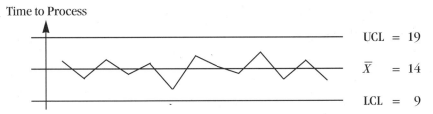

UCL = 19

$\overline{X}$ = 14

LCL = 9

Figure 2.24   Time to Process a Purchase Order

It seems like we have heard this before! Things were in-control, but not acceptable. No local faults were present. The old, tired, but typically proven unacceptable method of persuasion or threats to do better would have been useless. After the interdepartmental team did its job, it was found that the major system problem was confusing operating procedures leading to misunderstandings and errors that caused delays. These problems were corrected and the resulting average time to process an invoice was reduced to three days versus 14 days, and the plus or minus variability was reduced to one day, versus five days. The reduction in variability was considered as important as the lowered average value. Now to a different type of example.

In manufacturing, machine downtime is a very important variable, yet in some cases, poorly understood. Obviously, preventive maintenance and operator training are two major ingredients, both of which involve considerable common sense and experience in the typical firm. Operator training will be addressed specifically in later chapters. Now to the maintenance issue.

Just like any other variable in industry, downtime is subject to the same statistical vision of this chapter, and to the Deming philosophy. The same questions arise: Are there system problems manifested as chronic situations that local operators and mechanics are usually powerless to correct in a lasting fashion? Or is the major issue the existence of local faults indicating sloppy or inconsistent day-to-day situations that the local employees can probably identify? "Local" in this setting may involve the shift foreman. This is the person who is on the edge between "part of the system" and "a possible local fault." If he or she is part of poor supervision in general, a system problem exists and the control charts will probably show this. An isolated inadequate supervisor, however, is a local fault, and the control charts may indicate the nature of this issue as recurring, periodic bad situations when this person's crew is working. Of course, if upper management knows about this and tolerates the situation, perhaps one could still call it a system problem. But in any event, the control charts will eventually indicate the nature of the problem. Consider the following example in which supervision was not likely the problem.

A consumer products firm felt that it had excessive machine downtime, but for years was unable to identify any major causes. A control chart for total minutes of downtime across all categories was constructed for each department. Even after several months of chartroom analysis, no major findings emerged. Then, as part of an interdepartmental team, a mechanic suggested that since there were about 10 ways a machine could go down (stop), perhaps the high rates for some of the categories were canceling the lows for others within any given week. This was thus masking the true nature of the situation. Upon further discussion, this suggestion gained even more credibility, for several reasons. For one, if an operator and/or mechanic were struggling with a single type of machine problem, when the machine was down for this reason, the other categories of downtime could not occur. The machine was already not running. The minutes of downtime from the automated packager would be high this week; the tally for the other categories would be low and thus cancel out the culprit when total (summed) downtime was reported at the end of the period. Hence, in statistical terms, there was too much averaging.

At this time historical data were used to generate downtime control charts for each of the 10 categories. A typical control chart is shown in Figure 2.25 for the automated packager.

Minutes of Downtime

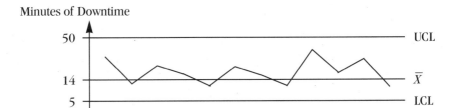

Figure 2.25   Downtime Control Chart for Automated Packager

The lack of symmetry of the chart is explained in Fellers (p. 52). The chart for the automated packager represented an in-control process. Upon analysis of this chart, the interdepartmental team determined the basic nature of the issue to be a system problem. As a review of an earlier chapter, they knew in advance that the following were likely true:

- It was an upper management issue.
- A formal interdepartmental team would be needed to make recommendations.
- It was an interdepartmental problem.
- It was a situation such that treating the issues as a local fault would demoralize people.
- An expensive solution was required.
- A long-term project was needed to correct the problem.

After many months of discussions and statistical analysis, it was found that the nature of the problem was too many vendors of corrugated boxes. All the suppliers were within specifications, but different. As the automated packager was fed boxes from a different vendor, which happened several times a day, it would jam and shut down the process. Or almost as bad, the operators would have to slow the machine down for an hour or so while they adjusted the automated packager (robot). These machine slowdowns did not even show up in our data. (The most important figures are unknown or unknowable!) Pareto charts (see page 36), defect per unit charts for each vendor (see page 52), and many plant visits enabled the team to pare down the number of suppliers from eight to two. The two remaining vendors were called partners and treated almost as part of the same company as we began to solve "our" problems together. Quality, costs, and service all reached heretofore unheard-of levels. This is what Deming calls the extended process, or thinking beyond the internal system. The extended process encompasses the system from the most basic raw material provider to the ultimate user. Until they all work as a team, total economies cannot be achieved. At the present in this country, the "potential" partners mostly fight it out through courts, lawyers, and corporate technocrats who designed the adversarial systems we are stuck with. Who wins? Not the stockholders, the regular employees, or the customers!

Back to the downtime example: The total process of problem recognition, issue resolution, and vendor selection took about 18 months. The corporate bureaucrats hated us every step of the way. They said that as long as a vendor was in-spec, we had no business discontinuing them or specifying how they run their factories. And furthermore, they said, the more vendors, the better. "Keep them hungry, off-guard, scared, receptive to price cuts, and honest," they said. In other words, treat them like dogs in an arm's-length, adversarial way! How could the corporate purchasing people have known? It was our fault, in a way, that they did not. We had failed to motivate upper management to grasp the statistical Deming vision. At the plant level, we were ultimately successful only because we were able to bypass corporate purchasing. Otherwise, this process improvement would have taken 10 years to implement, versus 18 months. At a more philosophical level, what was happening (and is everywhere) was that some of the corporate administrative overhead people were becoming unnecessary in the long term. With vendors and customers grasping the statistical vision and Deming philosophy, there is less need for corporate experts to clean up the legal and commercial administrative messes. In this case, if upper management vision had preceded our efforts by a year or more, they could (should) have dampened the corporate bureaucrats' fears by assuring them of continued employment somewhere else in the firm. Executives are very hesitant to make statements about guaranteed employment; so as in this case and many cases, we end up paying people to do useless (and often counterproductive) work for another decade or more. In defense of the corporate technocrats, hindsight is clearer than foresight, and the issues almost always seem clearer to an analytical outsider who does not have his or her vision clouded by politics and bureaucratic red tape. If the author had been the responsible corporate manager, the situation would have probably been much the same. Who am I to cast the first stone? But I wasn't the internal upper manager; I was an outsider looking for root causes. Now I've just told you about them. So listen and make something happen in your firm!

Back to the downtime issue again: There were 10 categories of machine stoppage problems. Most were in-control and fitted into the case of Figure 2.25. Several were out-of-control. For these few cases, temporary real-time control charts were used to help quickly identify the assignable causes. The interdepartmental team's first project involved helping correct these local faults to stabilize the process. This took about four months. Then with a mostly stable process, it was easier to address long-term system problems, such as troublesome vendors, lack of training, etc. There were fewer "fires to put out." None of the downtime control charts became permanent, on-line SPC tools. They were all temporary and for off-line analysis purposes. This practice is highlighted here to shed light on a basic misconception about SPC for nonproduct quality variables. A cumbersome chart may be only for temporary analysis purposes, and in some cases only historical data are used. Many would-be SPC practitioners have delayed starting for years because they feared having dozens of charts to be plotted permanently, many of which obviously have no real-time use.

Before leaving this section relating to maintenance, another chart that can be useful is discussed: the MTBF chart. The behavior of times between failures (occurrences) can help a manager distinguish between system problems and local faults. It can be shown that if a system is in-statistical-control, only two after-the-fact inspection procedures are theoretically sound. These are inspect every unit, or check none at all. In other words, sampling is either ineffective or inefficient.[15] The author was involved in a case where the operators visually inspected a piece from every unit (stack) of sheets that came off a corrugated box machine. This was about 1 percent inspection. The inherent scrap in this destructive testing cost about $80,000 per year, not counting the operators' time performing the tests. Product failures did occur, even though infrequently, so management was hesitant to discontinue the after-the-fact testing. For several weeks, the time of every product failure was recorded, a mean-time-between-failure (MTBF) chart was created, and the process was shown to be in-statistical-control. Consequently, it was decided to discontinue sampling and to form an interdepartmental team to improve the system. The 1 percent sampling was like "finding a needle in a haystack." Why bother? Spend this money to "prevent the presence of needles," upstream in the process. (Before embarking on an SPC analysis relating to MTBF, occurrences, and fractional sampling, it is important to refer to Gitlow (p. 48) and Fellers (p. 52). There are many infrequent, but nuisance-type occurrences that could be subjected to this MTBF analysis consisting of an SPC chart in combination with a review of the sampling plan, and if necessary, an interdepartmental team. Examples include:

- Mail misplaced.
- Calls misdirected.
- Employee absences.
- Injury occurrences.
- Crime occurrences.
- Electrical failures.

Why do we have so many opportunities remaining in the United States? Mostly because of our superstitiously trained leaders and teachers! They developed their management styles during a period when shortsightedness seemed to pay off. The world monopoly that the United States enjoyed in 1955 no longer exists. "Superstitiously trained" implies the learning of management tools during a period when the rules of the game were very different. An easy target for criticism are our business and engineering schools. Please be careful with your targeted criticism. The business systems and engineering practices of the United States are the envy of the world, even Japan. Our people have a work ethic approaching the best in the world. All that is universally missing is the statistical vision of the Deming philosophy, and this includes our business and engineering professors. The Deming SPC vision can be applied to almost any business variable that can be measured, or observed and classified. Appendix C is an excerpt from a list provided by Harrington.[16] There are many excellent administrative SPC candidates in this list. The statistical vision has been established, now here comes the accompanying Deming philosophy. Pay attention to the remaining chapters!

The issues in this book may seem very technical at times; however, we are really dealing with employee psychology. Curing the Deadly Diseases will create a conducive environment for heretofore unheard of teamwork. The author has seen few examples of good teamwork in industry, across about 100 client firms. No examples of perfect teamwork have been observed in the business world. In most situations people want to work as team members; we have a very strong social need to do just that. Just observe the typical guy outside his work environment. He joins groups, helps his neighbor work on his car, participates in Little League, etc. Why doesn't he do it at work? The major reason is the presence of some or all of the Deadly Diseases, to be discussed in the next five chapters. These diseases rob us of the creative spirit, our esprit de corps, our pride, our energy, etc. Many firms have all the diseases. All firms have some of them at times, hidden from insightful upper managers.

3
THE BIG PICTURE

Unlike many books about the Deming transition, this one will revolve around the Deadly Diseases, which are the deep-rooted problem. In contrast, other writers have organized around the 14 Points, which are action items intended to alleviate the Deadly Diseases. As a brief introduction the original Five Deadly Diseases are listed in Table 3.1. Chapters 4 through 8 will address each disease separately, and in detail. Also explained in each of these chapters are some of the 14 Points that should aid in the cure of the related disease. Explicit implementation plans will be provided.

Table 3.1   Original Five Deadly Diseases

1. Bottom-line management, mostly by visible figures alone.
2. Organized performance appraisal resulting in rankings, forced quotas, and many grading categories.
3. Lack of constancy of purpose.
4. Short-term approach of American managers.
5. Mobility of management.

As each disease is discussed at length in later chapters, keep in mind that our industry leaders are neither stupid nor ignorant (in most cases). They were superstitiously trained, or schooled by someone who was similarly trained prior to the emergence of our international competitors. Anything worked during the 1950s and 1960s because there was very little international competition at that time. Consequently, a short-term orientation developed in most firms. It seemed to make good sense back then to often forego process and product development to prop up the quarterly bottom-line, because this was the only report card. For a while, we did not feel overseas competitive pressures. For cultural reasons, and because some of them were under the influence of Dr. Deming and others, many of our international competitors were taking a considerably different approach, which is, of course, the subject of the rest of this book. At the risk of oversimplification at this point, one can generalize and state that our competitors were more willing and able to forego quarterly profits to reinvest more in their futures than we were in America.

When studying the Five Deadly Diseases in Table 3.1, one would think that it would be simple enough for upper management to just order everyone to stop doing these things. As you will see in subsequent chapters, if everyone in the firm obeyed, this would eventually enable the company to produce more effectively and efficiently in the long and short term. It seems this simple "stroke of a pen" approach is never taken, however, and for many good reasons I am sure. For one, upper managers never really have complete control over the day-to-day actions of the operational managers, regardless of what you hear. Another good reason is that upper management knows that some of these diseases are cultural sacred cows. Culture changing is the "talk of the town" these days; however, most top executives know that cultural changes come over many years of upper management's leading by example and through retirements. The new generation of managers entering the work force (under the age of 30) seems to be less likely to fall into the Deadly Disease trap. The examples that upper management must create for the older group will come largely through the 14 Points (listed in Appendix A for later reference). (Each will be discussed at length in subsequent chapters.) Adoption of these

14 Points will eventually rid the firm of the Deadly Diseases. When the entire work force acquires the statistical vision of Chapter 2 through adoption by management of the 14 Points, the Deadly Diseases cannot exist for long.

Why are the Deadly Diseases so bad? The most obvious technical reason is that the extreme short-term approach short changes process development, training, marketing research, and all those other good things that are necessary to compete in the long term. Most top executives in the past have expressed that against their will, this short-term orientation has been pushed on them by the ruthless institutional investors on Wall Street, who have no real interest in the companies in their portfolio. There is certainly some truth to this. However, the MIT Commission cited by Detouzous and Lester in Chapter 1 and the wide contrast among successful American firms void of the diseases with those marginal companies with most of the diseases certainly show that public pressure is a small part of the total problem.

Another more basic and important reason the Deadly Diseases are so horrible pertains to basic human nature. Consider the traits of the employees who would likely lead to the firm's becoming a world-class competitor. A partial list is provided in Table 3.2.

Table 3.2   Intangible Traits Needed to Be World Class

Creativity
Energy
Inquisitiveness
Desire to work for the good of the team
Eagerness to compensate for co-workers' shortcomings
Willingness to achieve results that are necessary, but unnoticeable to the boss

We will call the traits of Table 3.2 the "intangibles" throughout this book. Assuming there is adequate technical knowledge, which is usually easy enough to buy and generally superb in the typical American firm, possession of the intangibles will make the firm world class. Considering the statistical vision of Chapter 2 and how management overcontrol can demoralize the employees, one can begin to see why the Deadly Diseases have all but erased the intangibles in the typical American firm. Most of the Deadly Diseases involve a lack of statistical vision pertaining to variability and management's holding employees responsible for system common cause that is beyond their control. The result is a cadre of many burned-out employees possessing few of the intangibles. There is seldom energy to work as a true team, even if the employees knew how.

Adoption of the 14 Points of Appendix A, with the statistical vision to rid the firm of the Deadly Diseases, will eventually restore the intangibles. How long will this take? Three years in an idealistic case under close direction of a statistical master, 15 years for many firms awaiting the retirement of the superstitiously trained managers who do not want to hear about the new approach, and five to 10 years in the average case. There are Obstacles identified by Dr. Deming that will slow your progress (see Appendix B). The relevant Obstacles will be discussed in each upcoming chapter on the Deadly Diseases.

Now we will move on to a detailed analysis of each of the Five Deadly Diseases, the relevance of the 14 Points to help provide a cure, and the Obstacles that one can expect to encounter. The "glue" that will hold your efforts together and provide continuity is the statistical vision of Chapter 2 and the understanding that the adoption of each of the 14 Points is to rid the firm of a specific Deadly Disease(s). Keep your goals in mind. The author has seen many fragmented programs of adopting the 14 Points that were all inefficient, and only partially effective. Remember, the Deadly Diseases are the problem, the 14 Points are helpful cures, and the Obstacles are those stumbling blocks that almost always occur. Be ready to present convincing arguments, facts, and/or data to organization members who will present the Obstacles to you. Bless their little ignorant hearts! How could they have known? Their mentors and teachers were all superstitiously trained!

4

MANAGEMENT BY-THE-NUMBERS DEADLY DISEASE 1

Dr. Deming has made the statement in seminars, "Manage your firm solely by-the-numbers, and in five years, you will have neither numbers nor a firm to worry about." Obviously, practically no one manages solely by the numbers; however, a few extremely competent and insightful executives known by the author pay no short-term attention to the numbers at all. (When it comes to exerting pressure on the work force, that is.) Their organizations perform superbly. For most of us the issue here is to be at the correct place in the middle of these extremes, with a process to move closer to the more effective, intuitive approach of not relying on the numbers at all when it comes to motivating employees. As you will see in this chapter, too much emphasis on the numbers and the bottom line, in the short term, is a questionable practice that generally strangles all the intangibles from the work force. At best, but probably not at all, you will only get what you measure, and nothing else. As Dr. Deming has quoted eminent statistician, Dr. Lloyd Nelson, many times, "The important figures are often unknown and unknowable." Here are some examples of the unknown and unknowable:

- The future value of a satisfied customer.
- Pride of workmanship.
- The free publicity of a satisfied customer.
- Future value of enhanced teamwork.
- Reduced costs of stress-related illnesses.
- Improved quality for issues with no specifications.
- More safety.
- Self-satisfaction of a job well done.
- Better teamwork.

A bit of research was performed on the unknown and unknowables. Here are some typical examples that were meticulously quantified:

1. Across consumer products in general, a satisfied customer tells an average of eight people. A dissatisfied customer complains to 22.[17] The author tells about 1,000 receptive students and clients, and anyone else who will listen, about his getting "shafted." Just try me!

2. A satisfied car owner buys an average of four more of the same product over the next 12 years. They tell an average of eight people. The driver who bought the lemon tells an average of 16 people.[18]

3. You hear from less than 4 percent of your dissatisfied customers, but 91 percent never come back.[19] Customer complaints as the major source of feedback is very ineffective.

4. As reported by Peters and Waterman, it costs five times as much to acquire a new customer through advertising (and you may not keep the customer) than it does to retain customers through improvements in quality and customer service.

5. Based on a sophisticated statistical regression analysis, for every $1 reduction in external failure costs, $5.50 is added to the bottom-line profit.[20]

6. Any quantifiable cost savings or profit increase resulting from quality improvements can be multiplied by a factor of five to 10 to encompass the favorable unknowns and unknowables. (Bill Bern of Weyerhaeuser in Omaha, Nebraska, has proof of this. Ask him!)

Items 1 through 6, and others, certainly apply to your firm. What you cannot measure is always more important than what you can quantify. There are no exceptions! (Read the last two sentences again!)

While working in a paper mill once to help them implement SPC, an interesting comment from the production operators was noted. After a brainstorming session, when all the managers had left, a group of operators explained that the troubled labor relations of the past had little to do with the vocalized issues of pay, benefits, and security. These items were the "tip of the iceberg!" The true problem, which "ate at them" every hour of the day, was management's making them ship marginal product because the budgeted production (quota) for the day had to be met. There was no pride of workmanship! It was a disturbing, stinking place to work. In general, the research supports the fact that the most unhappy workers are the ones in the sleaziest organizations. According to Larson and La Fasto, they were disgusted at being asked to do things they did not feel good about. Only more pay and benefits can seemingly neutralize this problem. The operators of the paper mill sought more administered security because they feared (knew) that eventually many discerning customers would be lost. This experience was not an isolated case for the visitor to this firm. This situation exists in many firms!

There have been a number of interesting approaches to management (all somewhat appropriate, especially in their day) from more humane supervisory techniques (Mayo) to higher wages (Taylor), to more explicitly articulated objectives (Drucker), to emotional rallying of the troops (Peters).[21] With only a few exceptions, avid adoption of each of these seemingly promising approaches has yielded surprisingly unimpressive results. The same has occurred lately as many firms have been trying to implement SPC and total quality management (TQM) tools. Time and time again as the author was "in the trenches" and having difficulty trying to implement obviously good quality control or productivity enhancing tools, the deep-rooted underlying problem almost always turned out to be the strict adherence to the quotas, budgets, production, or sales targets. Hence, management by-the-numbers.

I know I have not made believers out of the by-the-numbers "diehards" yet. The statistical vision follows. Perhaps this re-statement by Deming will give you some insight. According to Dr. Nelson, "The central problem in management and productivity is failure to understand variation." Consider the simple example below in light of the statistical vision of Chapter 2.

The mill manager of a large paper mill expressed that he wanted 1,500 tons per day from the paper machines. This was a seemingly admirable goal because it had been infrequently accomplished in the past and because the company that sold them the machines told them that this was possible. (And we know a salesman would never stretch the truth.) It was difficult to get the operations personnel interested in long-term quality or productivity improvements because every day was a struggle, and they still rarely reached their 1,500 ton quota. The people had many opportunities to feel bad about themselves, and toward the company. Eventually a control chart was constructed using several months of historical data. Notice in Figure 4.1 that prior to point A, when there was constant pressure to do the impossible, the average was about 1,400 and the variability was manifested as a nonrandom, large, up-down-up-down motion. Hence, the infamous knee-jerk existed.

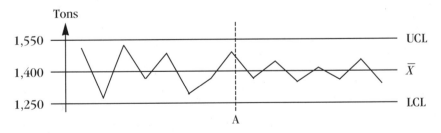

Figure 4.1   Tons per Day In-Control

At the request of a visionary, at point A, the pressure for 1,500 tons daily was relaxed. (There is one month purposely omitted after point A. It took some time for the supervisors and operators to believe that they would not [again] be chastised at the infamous 8 A.M. morning meeting for not meeting the daily quota.) The plot to the right of point A is typical. After the quota was removed, they still got the same average production level because the corporate culture and American way inherently led them to the "more is better" philosophy. This is not too bad when statistical vision is present. The most interesting phenomenon was that the large swing resulting from the knee-jerk response was greatly attenuated when the pressure to meet daily quotas was relaxed. The new control limits would be about 30 percent tighter than the original ones. With less demoralizing pressure to meet quota, the same average output and less variability resulted. (A proportional reduction in all inventories was now possible.) It was clear that the process was now in a state of statistical control and that the remaining random variability was mostly common cause. In other words, to move the average upward and to reduce the variability in a lasting fashion would require an insightful interdepartmental team approach. The plus or minus knee-jerk response prior to point A was from alternating "squeaking wheels." I can hear the comments at the infamous morning meetings now (in fact, I did hear them and took notes!):

"Got to have more production!"
(At the expense of preventive maintenance, quality checks, safety, etc., the machines were speeded up.)

Then the next day: "Scrap is up, QA is failing rolls, the converting department (customer) is complaining! We must do better!"
(The machines were slowed down and serviced properly and quality and good manufacturing processes were adhered to.)

The next day: "Got to have more production! How many more times do I have to say this?"

Ad nauseam! (My ulcer is burning and my heart is palpitating!)

After many years of demoralizing demands on the flustered operators and supervisors, it looks like the superintendent would have let up. To make matters even worse, the knee-jerk response of continually changing the machine speed yielded an output product with differing quality characteristics. The customers had always complained of this. Quality was improved by discontinuing the management by-the-numbers (quota). The production variability was less, thus enabling a proportional reduction in raw material and finished-goods inventory; but far more important, the employees were not being demoralized because management was no longer treating system common causes as local faults. They had owned up to the basic issue after the statistical vision sank in. The employees eventually had the energy to attack the real system problems. Now they had time to pay attention to quality, to look at the product, and to enhance customer satisfaction.

The message of this chapter is that the use of numerical objectives in a normal business setting is a horrible approach to managing people. A major reason for its ineffectiveness is the infamous knee-jerk response discussed above. Are all numerical goals bad? Of course not. A community goal of $500,000 for the United Way is not bad. This is not the normal business setting. There are no quality-quantity tradeoffs to elicit the knee-jerk response.

Now, how does the 1,500-tons-per-day example address the fallacy of management by-the-numbers. What do you give the foremen as numerical goals? As in the old days, 1,500 tons per day? Of course not, as just explained. This elicits a destructive knee-jerk response and uses up a tremendous amount of energy as the operators try to accomplish the impossible. When the boss came on strongly to indicate that 1,500 tons per day had been achieved in the past (even though it was a common cause, non-repeatable occurrence), few employees were willing to speak up and say, "I can't do it. I do not know how." It is not in our culture to accept defeat without a fight. (Remember John Paul Jones!) Consequently, goals not based on statistical vision are dangerous. This energy could otherwise be directed through the interdepartmental team to help management discover the system problems. Returning to management by-the-numbers, do you make the natural process average of 1,400 tons per day the objective (quota)? Of course not! This statement accepts defeat in that we do not expect to ever do better. What is the goal? We all must have goals! I suppose this is true, but not numerical ones in the absence of statistical vision. In this case, the yearly goals may be qualitative and something like this:

1. See that the relevant people get sufficient training to understand SPC and the statistical vision. (The training must be by a master.)
2. With some statistical guidance, construct an SPC chart to see the statistical nature of the problem.
3. If out-of-control, set up a real-time SPC procedure to help identify and correct the local faults. Consider using the problem-solving tools of Chapter 2 to help identify the vital few variables. Pareto charts are a must.
4. When (or if) in-statistical-control, establish an interdepartmental team to tackle the system problems. (By now it would be midyear, or later.) Report on the team members and the modus operandi of the team. Also, suggest any initial training needed.
5. Stay in touch with upper management pertaining to budgetary constraints and priorities. The upcoming recommendations must be reasonable.
6. Bring a prioritized list of action items from the interdepartmental teams to upper management. Take care of routine items as a team. (By now it is year-end. Items can be presented to upper management, but not all at once if some big hitters emerge early.)
7. Set up a control chart procedure to track your progress and to contrast the before and after. Every drop of improvement is celebrated!

These are the types of absolutely necessary things that for now are not likely to occur without some prodding by upper management. There is already a more is better mentality; generally speaking, this is certainly not bad. (In the general business sense, about the only effective universally acceptable long-term goal is market share, which encompasses everything: productivity, costs, quality, and service.) Granted, it may be necessary at times to do something drastic to stay in business. For example, to cut costs by 15 percent within two years. However, simple pressure and threats to "just be there" are totally ineffective. The people are mostly doing their perceived best. If costs must be cut by 15 percent, create the qualitative short-term objective of interdepartmental team formation. Ask the team to provide you a road map and a non numerical control strategy to see that it is followed. There must be many projects begun to achieve the 15 percent cost reduction. Never tell the corporate players that "you must do better." It never achieves lasting results.

These qualitative objectives can be audited just as the 1,500 tons per day can, but here we get at the true nature of the problem and attenuate the nasty variability-causing knee-jerk response. The employees will eventually regain their pride of workmanship. This takes about two years or longer. Two years may seem like forever in our short-term oriented society, but it is not. Most of these system problems have been around for 10 to 20 years. The pressure tactics have not made (and will not make) lasting improvements under the influence of a management by-the-numbers, bottom-line approach. System problems take time to solve; own up to it! According to Ryan, research shows that fewer than two-thirds of employees trust their immediate managers, and it will take time for the wounds to heal. When you ask for the impossible for years and make people's lives difficult for system problems beyond their control, they do not respond immediately when things change. For some truly humanistic, but superstitiously trained managers, if they knew the actual pain and suffering they had caused (or let happen), they would certainly be horrified. According to Levering, the National Institute of Safety and Health recently stated that the stress related to the lack of control over people's jobs contributes to heart disease, ulcers, and depression. The estimated yearly cost of these job-related stress illnesses is $450 billion, or about the same amount as our trade deficit. Another study across 500 firms showed that the work stress resulting from no control over the job creates the same risk as heavy smoking or an elevated serum cholesterol level. When you manage by-the-numbers through quotas, MBO, etc., there will always be competing objectives for different people that create unnecessary stress and demolish teamwork. This is simply not necessary and is generally a sign that the manager does not understand the process well enough to get involved in helping improve it. Will these superstitiously trained managers who treat system problems as local faults have to answer for these deaths on Judgment Day? Probably not because we have a just God. "How could they have known?" They couldn't have, but if you are reading this book, you know now, so quit it!

To quote Deming, "Work standards, piece rates, and quotas are manifestations of inability (or unwillingness) to understand and to provide appropriate supervision." To be a bit more blunt, sole and heavy use of numerical objectives as a management tool may signal a deep problem within the manager. It may be motivational in that he or she just wants to "get things off my desk." And at least for a while after espousing numerical goals, everything seems rosy, until the year-end returns come in. In other words, the manager does not want to be bothered with the process of making a product or providing a service. Pertaining to the typical paper mill case, as an example, when you look at the seven qualitative objectives above to replace the ignorant use of a numerical quota, you can see that there is no such thing as a universal professional manager. Management is not easy! You have to be there, to know the process, to get your hands dirty, to understand the issues, and to set examples. In other words, manage in much the same ways that your grandfather would have. In his day, before the fluke post World War II era of superstitious learning when we temporarily had a world monopoly, there were no elaborate management systems like MBO, work quotas, budgeted targets, etc. People just stayed close to the business and paid attention. To quote Tom Peters, "The best managers are avid notetakers. They are shameless thieves!" In other words, they pay attention! As discussed in Larson and La Fasto, to quote Duke Drake who most successfully turned around Dun & Bradstreet, "This stuff about being lonely at the top is a bunch of B.S. If you're lonely at the top, you are not doing your job." Insightful, effective administrators manage by being there, by paying attention, and by setting examples. You cannot delegate your job away by simply establishing numerical performance objectives! (If you can, let me know about it, and I will program my personal computer to do your job at half your salary.) The Deming statistical vision has given us a way to quantify the obvious: the system will only do what it can do, until we change it. Only upper management can change it. How? Get the statistical vision, form interdepartmental teams, get involved in the process, and stop trying to motivate with the by-the-numbers approach. Management mostly by-the-numbers never works! Even if you can get what you measure, which is unlikely, you get nothing else. Most of the important issues are immeasurable. At routine production or sales meetings, there must be little or no discussion of yesterday's or last week's figures. This is management by-the-numbers, regardless of what you call it. The dyed-in-the-wool, by-the-numbers people are often defensive and retaliatory to those who cross them. This is a cover-up (perhaps subconscious) for their lack of process knowledge and for their simply not having the slightest idea of what to do, except to announce numerical goals hoping someone will miraculously bail them out. It never happens, however. People only get demoralized. I can hear them now, "Last year was not good! Next year our goal is to improve by 5 percent." No plan, no road map, only misguided hope. Why not wish for 25 percent while you are at it? An experienced manufacturing vice president once stated that he had to commit to a 3 percent increase in production for next year to get his needed capital appropriations from upper management. Consequently, he had to use MBO to force his subordinates to provide this. Several comments apply. First, his initial statement may have been true. Second, why not ask for 4 percent, 5 percent, or 6 percent while wishfully pressuring the employees? Each makes about as much sense if there is no explicit road map for achievement or no scientific basis for the 3 percent increase. If there is a scientific justification to indicate that the capital improvements will yield a 3 percent increase, it will happen if we follow our plans. There's no need to jawbone and to threaten the employees. Third, as an insightful employee stated, the vice president had demanded a 3 percent increase every year for the last decade. The system never produced it. It looks like he would have given up on numerically based MBO.

The next related example pertains to budgeting. To the "man from Mars" peeking in on us, I am sure that he sees budgets as a time-consuming waste to cover up for organizational shortcomings and private agendas, but we all know they are a must in our society. Budgets, however, rarely accomplish their total objective. There are many reasons for this, but the one that permeates practically every situation observed by the author over 20 years is a lack of statistical vision and the consequential inability to decipher local faults from system issues. The basic problems thus seldom get solved because the participants do not know how to approach them by using simple control systems to identify local faults or interdepartmental teams for system problems. The latter is typically the issue. In any event, there are perennial budget deviations that the firm learns to live with as "the nature of the beast." This resulting lack of discipline because "we never meet budget" degrades the potentially useful purposes of budgeting. The net result is often a "big zero," and the firm would be just as well off not to budget in some areas at all. Let's look at an actual example. Consider Figure 4.2.

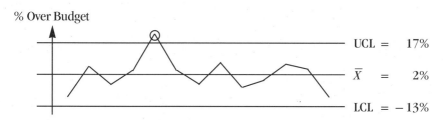

Figure 4.2   Generally Over Budget: System Problem

Figure 4.2 is a time plot for percent over budget in a depart-ment over 31 months. The same theory would apply if it were for 31 cost centers for a single interval. There was one out-of-control point that was easily reconciled. A seldom-used vendor accidentally labelled a drum of chemical incorrectly, which dissolved the seals of the local mechanical process and ruined an expensive equipment item. The statistically local fault was not a result of the local employees, but they easily were able to identify the assignable (special) cause. In this case, a control chart would not have enhanced their realization that the green fluid was oozing out of the seams; however, for analysis purposes at the next budgeting time, the after-the-fact chart could have been very useful. The point was that the normal system was in-statistical-control. There were no local routine faults, and the seemingly inattentive local employees for whom the budget was supposed to motivate to pay attention were unable to solve the system problem of typically being above budget. Remember the nature of system problems from page 18; only an interdepartmental team of some sort is likely to make lasting improvements.

From Figure 4.2 one can see that this cost center was on the average 2 percent above budget with an obvious, alternating plus minus 15 percent swing. High, then low. The infamous knee-jerk response. After a particularly bad month, needed expenditures were not made. You know the sort: The boss locks up the supply cabinet and people have to stay in sleazy hotels over the weekend on business trips to get the reduced over-the-weekend airfare rate. Then the percent over budget could actually swing negative on the next cycle, thus under budget. Then pent-up demand for paper clips and the desire to fly back home on Friday night to visit with the three-year-old daughter would cause people to go "hog wild" to force things to swing back in the unfavorable direction on the next cycle. On a more serious track, there were variable operating needs that also caused the successive months to be different.

The interdepartmental team found that the basic system problems were two-fold. First, the budgeting process was intermingled with the setting of the yearly performance objectives for quantifiable items, which in itself is totally invalid unless under the close scrutiny of expert statistical vision (if then). So department heads felt compelled to present themselves a challenge for the boss. With no road map or understanding of why costs were excessive last year, how could one plan to spend less next year at the same operating level (adjusting for inflation, of course)? Consequently, on the average everyone was subsequently 2 percent over budget. All the pressure in the world to meet the budget objective would have provided no lasting improvement unless there also was a statistical vision by upper management. The downside did occur. People were flustered and the budgeting process lost credibility.

The second problem was the department manager's treating of common cause budget variances as local faults leading to the knee-jerk response discussed earlier. Part of the plus-or-minus 15 percent variability of Figure 4.2 was from the system problem of overcontrol. When this behavior by the department head was discontinued, it was later established that the true operational common cause variability was plus-or-minus 10 percent (versus 15 percent). As a new operational procedure, a monthly control chart was maintained for percent over budget. Unless there was a statistically significant out-of-control deviation (see the four cases on page 10), no action was to be taken by the department head. Then there was energy and motivation available to tackle some real cost cutting endeavors, versus the unnatural knee-jerk response of the past. Morale improved and the employees began letting the boss "play in their reindeer games" again. The boss no longer seemed like a number-crunching person of no vision.

The word that seems dear to most upper managers these days is "teamwork." They have noticed that most remaining problems in their firms are system problems, and thus interdepartmental teams are required to enhance teamwork. Management by-the-numbers normally destroys teamwork! It's every person for himself or herself! Tom Watson, former CEO of IBM, stated it very well: "The 80s had plenty of individual business heroes [mostly corporate raiders]. In the 90s the winners will be entire companies that have developed cultures that, instead of fearing the pace of change, relish it." [22] Managing by-the-numbers, whether it be a formal disgusting system like MBO, or less structured, is ruining teamwork in most firms. Survival in the short term occupies all the thought processes. It is impossible to establish perfectly coordinated numerical objectives for all the players. There will be seemingly competing objectives like production, quality, scrap, preventive maintenance, and training. Even in the best of cases when all numerical objectives are achieved (which the author has yet to see unless the goals were so unchallenging that they were the laughing stock), the firm will eventually crumble because of the deterioration of the intangibles and unknowables. Winston Churchill made an interesting statement when he said, "Each person only has to do his duty to wreck the world." What Churchill was referring to was the fact that without the synergies of teamwork, very little of lasting benefit will be accomplished. One of the most publicized advocates of management by-the-numbers was the late Harold Geneen of ITT. The historical record certainly supports the fact that it seemed to work well for him in the 1950s and 1960s, but the unknowables were causing his firm to "rot at the seams," with no one aware of it at the time. When Geneen left, there was not sufficient teamwork and synergy to keep the place going at the same level of profitability. The firm's success has never been the same since he left.

According to Pascale and Athos, the Japanese people are cultured from birth to be team players and to exercise constraint when judging others. Grading a subordinate as pass/fail based on meeting a numerical goal would be very distasteful to a Japanese manager. The comparative issue is not that they never got into the manage by-the-numbers, bottom-line, "tail wagging the dog," management style because they were smarter than Americans. They did not dare try it! It would have been a cultural taboo. It worked for us for a while during the 1950s and early 1960s only because of the fluke monopoly for American goods following World War II. Then, around 1967, the intangibles and unknowables caused the world to begin crumbling around us. (As early as 1959 in some markets.) Also, we embraced the bottom-line approach because we were cultured to be individualistically rugged. I can hear John Wayne now: "Get the cards out on the table, boy!" Perhaps this was okay in the days of expanding frontiers, and no international competition, but not now. There will be few corporate heroes in the future, only successful team players. Teamwork involves compensating for others' weaknesses. It is difficult to do this when you have to meet quotas that lack statistical vision.

Are quotas always unrealistically high? Of course not! Sometimes they are unrealistically low, but equally as demotivating. A student at Augusta College revealed once that he had been a salesman and was expected to sell $6,800 worth of goods per week, and this was generally a very easy task. He did it by Tuesday and took a five-day week-end most of the time. He revealed that if he had been treated like an adult with no quota he would have sold 50 to 75 percent more. The sales people were all afraid to beat the quota because their superstitiously trained managers would have raised it. Then they would have been forced to work at someone else's pace, and not their own. Another student who worked for a utility company stated that he had a quota of meters to read every day, and as he read them the figures had to be keyed into a gadget that electronically transmitted the numbers back to the office along with the exact time of entry. This was so that he could be audited to enable management to make sure he worked all day. It would have been easier and cheaper to simply log the figures the old fashioned way, but management did not like the old system. They did not know how to manage these meter readers. It was too easy for the meter readers to finish their quota early in the day and then goof off. What the meter readers started doing was to log the numbers the old way on a scratch pad and then every three minutes while at the lake fishing or resting at home later in the afternoon, they would transmit the next number. He said they could not let management know that the job could be completed in an average of five hours per day. They would raise the quota proportionally and this would not work, because on a truly bad day, it took almost eight hours to do the job. (Rain, irritated dogs, heat, and sickness were contributors to truly bad days.) This student meter reader said that in the absence of a quota and in the presence of being treated like an adult, the productivity would have increased at least 25 percent. Consider the following typical example where what you hear is only the "tip of the iceberg," or perhaps not anywhere near the real issue.

A utility company was having intense labor unrest for the first time in many years. Management was at first confused. There seemed to be no reason other than the normal pay and benefits suggestions offered by the field technicians. In other words, nothing seemed new! A person schooled in the Deming philosophy eventually got to the bottom of the issue. As this person found, to put pressure on the field technicians to hustle more, the edict came down from corporate headquarters that all technicians' objective was to make five services every day, and all variances were to be dealt with by the immediate supervisor. The foolish management by-the-numbers objective was five per day. This was an everyday expectation, not 25 per "week" to enable the random high and low days to cancel out. Also, to make matters worse, on some days one-hour jobs were the norm, other times a single job may take all day. Quality did not enter in. The technicians began turning in partially completed work orders stamped "completed" (that's all that counted) knowing the customer would complain later. This made the technicians feel nauseated to have to lie to survive in this environment. Their pride of workmanship was stolen from them. Not only was there no prior statistical determination made to evaluate the common cause variability, the quota of five per day was even invalid, as a daily average. A hotshot 25-year-old corporate fast-burner came up with the number "five" by riding one (that's right, one) day with a technician. Who knows if the repairs made that day were typical or not. There was no professional industrial engineer present who was trained in work sampling. Also, the transient time around the big city was probably a tenth of the normal distance between calls in this predominantly rural state. Each territory covered many miles except in the one densely populated city. At last check, this problem has still not been solved. At the outset I am sure the young technocrat was able to calculate many millions of dollars of projected yearly savings. (Can't wait for his next favorable performance appraisal!) The hotshot fast-burner was keeping the real truth from the corporate higher-ups. (Mr. Big in this company, please be reading this book. You will know it's you I am talking to.) What should have been done in this case instead of setting a quota of five per day? Probably nothing! The utility was noted already for superb service. Perhaps create interdepartmental teams to establish legitimate recommendations, such as better manuals, more effective dispatching, etc. In general, if you try to set statistically untested quotas to cover up for your failure to understand the real process and to hide your inability to lead it toward continual improvement, the world will "crumble from under your feet." The problem is that the relief valve often appears in the most unusual places, and by this time the real culprit often has already exited the scene. A control chart of service calls completed per day would have shed some light on this problem. Can you begin to see why managing by-the-numbers, with no statistical vision, can (and usually will) be devastating?

Some managers say that the quotas must be replaced with something. Is this true? Probably not, with the exception of a statistical determination of the state of the system and perhaps some interdepartmental teams that provide the vision to get started improving the system. If the employees are not ready for this, start the training and nurturing now. Let them first see you start to destroy the Deadly Diseases, by example.

Teamwork cannot flourish well in the presence of numerical goals and no statistical vision. Without the by-the-numbers disease, teamwork is at least possible. Will it automatically flourish across the entire organization when this Deadly Disease is cured? No, but teamwork has a chance, for a change.

A supervisor once stated that if he used fear tactics, he could meet most any short-term production quota. It seemed to some that he could. Numbers can at times temporarily be held at a seemingly impossible level, but somewhere there is a "release valve" if you are beyond the system capabilities. In America, the hidden price we pay is usually in poor quality or burnout of the work force rendering them uninterested in improving the system. For the firm in question we did a correlation study of customer credits (money back) versus time. There was almost a 100 percent correlation between excessive customer credits and the periods in which the supervisor was involved in one of his "production-at-all-costs" drives. This is a typical case. The unknowables were sacrificed for short-term gains. There was no energy to continually improve or to be concerned about customer satisfaction. Are there exceptionally critical cases where a very strong, by-the-numbers, short-term approach is warranted? The answer is yes, but the incidence of such cases is so rare that it is hardly worthy of mention. If a new incoming plant manager has one year to drastically turn around a facility to prevent the loss of jobs and to protect company investment, the long-term issue does not exist unless the short term is salvaged. Two issues come to mind. First, management should announce that this short-term, by-the-numbers approach is temporary for immediate survival. Once in the "black," a more creative long-term approach will be practiced. This announcement keeps the survival tactics from becoming too deeply rooted in the culture. The second empirical observation is that the typical emergency situation exists because of a historical by-the-numbers orientation. No intangibles present and no continual improvement of system problems caused the predicament. I think this is the reason why firms who have discontinued the strong by-the-numbers approach seem to never have to revert to their old ways. Consider the example below where an honest attempt to do better by using a strong by-the-numbers approach actually could endanger people's safety.

A manufacturing vice president stated once that an analysis of safety statistics is a good way for a top executive to "see below the water level to make sure the tip of the iceberg was not deceiving him." What he meant was that if the operational managers were pushing too hard to meet the short-term numerical objectives, accidents were often the "release valve." One must be careful, however. A renowned statistician once said, "Be skeptical of all empirical data!" (The reference eludes me, but it was said.) Accident data will vary just like any other type. As with any chronological time-sequenced data to be analyzed, the summary interval must be wide enough so that each snapshot of time has an ample opportunity of being representative of the average situation. For example, one cannot keep a chart on average rainfall with a point plotted every day. This is because some days it does not even rain. A monthly or quarterly chart would be more appropriate. The same applies for accidents. Most days, even weeks, have no occurrences. The firm in question decided to plot accidents per million man-hours of exposure. The control chart is shown in Figure 4.3.

Note that at point A, the accident rate began to go out-of-control. There was a local fault and unlike most local fault issues, it would probably be extremely difficult to isolate. None of the managers

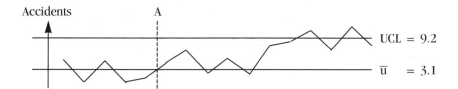

Figure 4.3   Accident Rate Going Out-of-Control

would talk; however, finally an hourly employee told a consultant that with the new daily quotas on production, safety guidelines had to be ignored. The quotas were, even in the best of cases, foolishly based on random good days from last year that could not consistently be repeated. The manufacturing director had recently started MBO, one of Deming's Deadly Diseases. And it backfired, as it always does! The "relief valve" was an increased accident rate.

An interesting example reported by Deming involves the Air Quality Index in the Los Angeles area. If it gets over 150, there has to be a lengthy investigation. What do you know? Every day it hovers right at 148 or 149. It is easy for a knowledgeable statistician to look at a plot of these data or to perform an analysis of the data and see that this supposedly random variable is not. Hold 'em to the numbers and they'll beat you some way! Fear causes lying! Consider another example from Neave.[23] Accidents at a nuclear site had been occurring at a rate of 12 per year. Upper management applied extreme pressure to cut the rate in half. It was done. Hazardous work was subcontracted to outside vendors whose accidents did not get counted. Results: same number of accidents or more, costs went up, upper management was temporarily pleased! Consider another example from the author's repertoire. A company president attended a seminar on JIT. A corporate technocrat convinced the president that zero inventories were a necessity for competitiveness, and soon. The edict came down, with no road map. Raw material inventories were to be reduced to zero, and immediately! What happened? The plants were nowhere near ready for JIT. Their responses varied and were all expensive and demoralizing. One plant manager, for example, would keep raw materials in the railcars, moving around the area, until he needed them. The holding costs were not accrued until the stuff was unloaded. The transportation costs were at least 10 times the savings from inventory carrying costs. If you are managing mostly by-the-numbers, there are many examples almost as bad existing in your firm. As another example, the author knows of an electronics firm that had monthly shipping quotas that had to be met, or your next bonus was jeopardized. Thirty percent of their monthly output was generally shipped on the last working day of the month. Immediately, service personnel were dispatched to the customers' sites to install missing parts or to fix the items. The plant management knew that most of the stuff shipped on the last day was defective. Costs were high, customers were unhappy, the plant managers got their monthly bonuses, upper management could not understand why quality was so bad, and the lower managers were reluctant to explain to the big bosses that their by-the-numbers management style was totally ineffective. Eventually the firm was forced out of business and a thousand families were disrupted.

The quotas in the absence of statistical vision generally elicit fear, not to mention the unexpected reactions and the accompanying nervous activity that sends the message to the boss that "at least I am doing something." The accompanying, needless mind chatter is a hamper to creative thought. There is no incubation period for your subconscious mind to sort out the issues. The author can look back on his hectic industry experience now, 15 years later, and visualize multimillion dollar, easy-to-implement improvements that he failed to see at the time. Dozens of successful retired executives have told him about the same type of experiences. Ask a few retirees to discuss their missed opportunities because of needless mind chatter resulting from short-term, nearsighted quantitative objectives. Lack of trust, fear, negative personal judgment, and perceived autocratic supervision are also major creativity destroyers. As discussed earlier, by-the-numbers management fans the flames of all these problems. Creativity among most of the organizational members is a must for survival into the next century. There are a number of reasons why it is largely nonexistent these days, and management by-the-numbers is at the top of the list. Everything begins to revolve around "pleasing the boss." The surest sign of a lack of teamwork is too much of the "make the boss look good" mentality. If the boss is the number one customer in the minds of most employees (not the real customer), the organization is headed for trouble. (Keep your resume updated! You will need a job within five years!)

Will gut feel and intuition eventually replace the void caused by the discontinuance of management by-the-numbers? It certainly will, and it's about time! "So-called" managers who cannot handle this will flee. Solid evidence indicates that those who rely most heavily on intuition make more profitable decisions than their by-the-numbers (systems) counterparts. Engineers John Mihalasky and E. Douglas Dean at the New Jersey Institute of Technology found that 80 percent of those company leaders who had doubled their profits in a five-year period had above average intuitive power scores on a battery of tests. Research has also shown that top managers in general, the ones who have made it, scored higher than the norm on intuitive powers.[24] The author has interviewed dozens of successful top managers about intuition versus "by-the-numbers." Practically all of them pay little attention to the numbers in the short term. They know! Who then are the manage by-the-numbers culprits? Frequently it is the middle management technocrats trying to make an impressive, quick showing to the big guys. The visionary upper managers must authoritatively stop this practice, but first provide nurturing and training in the Deming vision. Research by Ray and Myers showed that we only use about five percent of our creative ability. This figure would be 25 to 30 percent if all the by-the-numbers Deadly Diseases were eliminated.

How does the publicized technique called management by walking around (MBWA) fit with the Deming approach of not managing by-the-numbers? Not very well at times! Sure, intuition and gut feel can be accentuated by casually walking the halls. However, as soon as the manager starts asking questions with quantifiable answers, the knee-jerk response comes right back, even in the absence of a formal by-the-numbers system.

At another extreme, when there's a quota, there's often no incentive to do better. As an example, academia business school professors must publish a minimum of two refereed journal articles every five years to be counted as a publishing instructor at reaccreditation time. This is a rule by the American Association of Collegiate Schools of Business. Fifty percent of the professors at every college must get the "yes column" checked as it pertains to publishing for the college to maintain their accreditation. A few professors fast-burn to create a long list of publications to enable them to stay mobile within academic circles (another Deadly Disease if the deans as a group let this happen). Occasionally they publish extensively because of a deep sincere desire to do research. However, what does the typical professor do when he or she has a "hot streak" and completes more than the minimum two required every five years? They sandbag by withholding submittals to the journal editors until they need them to meet quota, unless of course a promotion milestone is eminent, which is a sort of quota. The net result? Less published research. What's the answer to this dilemma? I do not know. I am part of this system and "cannot see the forest for the trees" myself.

Can putting up a banner or a poster get people on track? Dream on! Consider the case of the hospital with a higher than industry average adverse patient outcomes (APO) level. An APO is a medical error like an unscheduled return to the operating room, or an incorrect drug taken. This variable was expressed as incidents per 1,000 patient days. Their average was nine, as shown in Figure 4.4. This example is similar to the one reported in Demos.[25]

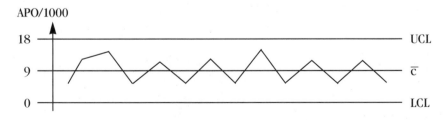

Figure 4.4   APO Control Chart

The hospital administrator put up posters and reminders all over the hospital as motivation tools. Several that come to mind were:

Zero Defects Is Possible

Safety Is Your Responsibility

Safety Pays

A Person's Life Is in Your Hands

Haste Makes Waste

Did things improve? Absolutely not. (I can hear the surgeon now, "Nurse, I believe I will be careful and not leave a scalpel inside this guy. Remember, safety pays!") As the control chart later showed, there were no local faults that simply paying closer attention would likely solve. An interdepartmental team was eventually formed to help solve some of the system problems. Only upper management could solve the types of problems found:

- Too few nurses.
- Nurse pay too low.
- Residents overly fatigued.
- Operating rooms poorly scheduled.

The author was recently entering the door of a potentially unsafe manufacturing plant about two steps behind two senior machine operators who were reading the infamous banner at the entrance:

Safety Pays

One operator whispered over to the other, "I sure am glad they reminded me of this. I had planned to stick my head into the concentrated sulfuric acid tank today. Now I think I will not do it." Banners are directed to the wrong people. The employees know this! Tear all banners and motivational posters down today and forbid them in the future. This includes many demeaning safety posters. Obviously, however, some signs have needed facts on them:

Women

Men

Hot

Danger

Police Line

Quicksand

Open Sewer (With Alligators)

Men Working

Deep Hole

Bad Dog

Do not take these signs down. Perhaps put this sign up:

Leave Brains Here at Front Door:
Superstitiously Trained Managers Inside

Have you ever wondered why discrediting jawboning and threats seldom elicit the desired lasting improvements? Consider the following example.

Many operational managers are quick to criticize their customer service associates. You know, the people who have to continue to smile and to explain to the customers why and how the company plans to "do better." The phrase "do better" in this book is repeated for nauseating emphasis. Every time I have ever heard it in practice, it was a telltale sign of chronic system problems. No statistical vision, no interdepartmental understanding of the true nature of the problem(s), no road map for change; consequently, there is fear! Occasionally fear can give short-term results; however, with many ill side effects. It bleeds the creative spirit right from the hearts of the employees. The desired short-term results seldom last. The oftentimes implication from the manager is, "Get this issue off my desk; make my day; please, run my job for me; I do not understand the problem." Of course the manager does not understand the problem! It is multi-disciplined and beyond the perception of any one person. And there is no teamwork! Now back to the customer services department example.

Manufacturing executives often state that they have heard the customer services personnel "cry wolf" too many times. These guys report what seems to be isolated customer complaints, then upon investigation there is no problem with the manufacturing process. After mastering the statistical vision, the suspicion would be that the process is in-statistical-control; however, inherent to its natural state is the production of a few defective items. In the following case, the number of defects was so low, that trying to screen them out at the manufacturing plant was futile. This is what the author calls the "needle in the haystack" phenomenon. Furthermore, if it can be shown that the process is in a state of statistical control, only two after-the-fact inspection plans can be justified economically, as stated earlier: all or none. There's a formula in Gitlow and Gitlow to help one establish which extreme applies. Usually, the choice is obvious and "none." The real issue is to first understand the true nature of the problem, local faults or system problems, and then plan an approach to prevent the defects in the first place. You cannot find a needle in a haystack, even with a larger handful of straw, so one must figure out a method for making it impossible for the needle to be there in the first place. It is futile to waste your resources looking for the needle. Consider the control chart of Figure 4.5.

Figure 4.5   Defects per Shipment

A cooperative customer, who saw all the product, agreed to save all defective items for the vendor. The control chart in Figure 4.5 was constructed and showed a state of control. The one outlier was easily traced to a rare accident in the vendor's plant. What the control chart meant was that the problem(s) was a system issue, and treating it as a local fault was in the long term discrediting and demoralizing. The manufacturing people were defensive toward the customer services people for years before the statistical vision was presented, they had learned to fabricate white lies for customer service complaints. They did not want to alter the process in a short-term, knee-jerk fashion when they knew it was in-statistical-control. The author has named these white lies as "survival lies." The author has actually seen many cases where the survival lies were preestablished and agreed upon by the internal people. I can hear it now. The plant manager gets a call from customer service, "The XYZ Company is steaming. Another of our cartons shut down their process. Something must be done now! Tell me what we plan to do to correct the problem by 3 P.M. tomorrow!" The plant manager calls Joe down in process engineering who, knowing that this "needle" is inherent to the process, looks on his preestablished list, picks white lie number 32, and reports it back to the plant manager. The survival lie enables him to avoid process tampering and to get on with his job.

Referring back to Figure 4.5, the point is that the same process produced the good and bad items. When in-statistical-control, you cannot "catch it" making a bad one and thus easily correct the local fault. There is no local fault! What do you do? Lean on survival lies like many firms have been doing for so long? Of course not! Create a control chart to enhance your understanding of the problem. Then create an interdepartmental team to permanently improve the system. Measure your success. Praise and flaunt any statistically significant improvement, regardless how small. Then ask for a bit more.

The case above pertained to small cartons that housed a consumer product. Pareto charts (p. 37) on type of defect, day of month, and raw paper vendor indicated to the interdepartmental team that when a certain vendor's paper was used, and only by one carton shift crew, the problem arose. The problem was easily corrected. The major culprit reflected haphazard and poor training by the carton vendor. OJT had been the predominant training tool. The graveyard shift employees were the newest and had been poorly trained by Bill on the day shift as they followed him around for several days. Bill was a terrible choice for a coach. He complained all the time and did not entertain questions. Furthermore, as mentioned earlier, from the author's experience, OJT as a sole method of training is a horrible practice. The operators need the theory, the practical (ropes), and most important, a full understanding of the corporate mission pertaining to quality and continual improvement. (More will follow in later chapters on training and corporate mission statements.) How can you get a supervisor interested in training when he or she is only interested in the budget and in preventing boondoggles. You cannot in midyear when dealing with superstitiously trained supervisors. Obviously, his or her managers must be enlightened to include this need into next year's budget. As you will see when you grasp the total thrust of this entire book, the concept of budgeting will likely be changing over the years. For enlightened firms of the future, if opportunities to improve service, quality, or employee pride of workmanship surface in midyear, they will be implemented. The by-the-numbers, stick-to-the-budget approach is a dying dinosaur.

For the carton vendor of this case, it would have taken many months to start a formal training program, which they eventually did; in the meantime, however, several open brainstorming sessions among operators of all crews enabled most of the problems to be solved. The magic here was the interaction among crews from all three shifts. There was a resulting synergy: the whole was greater than the sum of its parts. Each operator crew had different pieces of the puzzle. Why had management not started these inter-crew brainstorming sessions before? They had, and called it quality circles, which failed miserably, as they have for 90 percent of the U.S. firms that tried them. The author could see three major reasons for the failure of the previous quality circle work groups. First, they were too formal and structured by the corporate technocrats. The operators saw them as the latest example of another management program, doomed for failure, because in reality all they wanted was for the operators to do better. In other words, too much ineffective fanfare. Second, when recommendations did come out of the meetings, management usually ignored them, and for several reasons. For one, the team leaders did not have the skills to keep impossible-to-implement suggestions off the list of recommendations. The $40 million new plant had been disapproved by corporate headquarters six times before. Why let it come up again! Third, and most important, about 10 times more energy was required to nurture the social side of these groups than the leaders provided. The members never began to have fun! What was needed was catered-in lunches during the meetings, breakfast meetings at the country club, cocktail hour, informal gatherings, family picnics, and the exclusion of a couple of killjoys. (Thanks to John Van Steenberg and Bill Mazur of Kimberly-Clark for teaching me this.)

It is easy to talk about prevention and zero defects, but extremely difficult to accomplish, and for many reasons, most of which are obvious to you. Some reasons are very difficult to uncover, however. They are deeply embedded within the system, they are multidisciplined, at times the random highs and lows cancel each other out, they take a long time to solve, plus patience and teamwork to correct. Even the hero-hopefuls have been ineffective to date. In the United States, the bureaucratic departmentalization, the lack of statistical vision, and the seemingly good, but disastrous, short-term, bottom-line approach, are preventing the typical firm from achieving its potential. The statistical vision has been presented in this book. Try to apply it in your day-to-day thought processes and to the rest of this book. The remaining chapters of this book provide a discussion of and a how to for the curing of the Five Deadly Diseases and the implementation of the 14 Points. Hence, the only efficient solution to this dilemma. In each section, new examples will be provided to enhance the connection with the statistical vision.

One last example from Latzko and a similar one espoused by a student follow. About 40 percent of the cost of operating the average bank can be attributed to errors, or the inspection required because of the potential for errors. Of this amount of money spent, only about 2 percent goes toward prevention. There are few interdepartmental teams that the author knows of; however, Latzko reports that in at least one case, an interdepartmental team reduced this cost to less than 50 percent of its original rate. An example reported by a student may help explain why the situation is so bad in some cases. This woman worked in the check clearing operation where the poor production rate and percent defective had not changed in many years. There was a weekly quota of checks that had to be processed, or according to some formula, the person responsible would be fired. There was considerable double and triple inspection. The employee turnover rate was high despite the good pay. The excessively high wage was to cover up management's unwillingness to address the basic issues. The student said that with no quota, the total cost of processing the checks would have been about 25 percent lower. Perhaps there would be a need for a few more workers, but almost no inspectors would be required. The employees were treated poorly with these quotas and thus did not have the time or energy to suggest opportunities for lasting improvement. Management knew not what to do, so they established quotas. The "old carrot and stick." How could management have known? It had its own MBO goals and quotas to thwart their intangibles and creative spirit. Obviously, the initial thrust for improvement should come from the top down, or at least two levels in the hierarchy above the local employees. After establishing a statistical vision, a percent defective control chart probably would have shown the process to be in-control, thus requiring an interdepartmental team to make recommendations to upper management. Possible recommendations (I am guessing at times here!) include the following:

- No quota (not a guess).
- No inspectors.
- More modern equipment.
- Fewer identified distractions.
- Eye tests.
- Control charts.

Over the next several pages a discussion follows for the 14 Points and Obstacles from Appendices A and B that are most applicable to the by-the-numbers disease. Since you have the statistical vision by now some of these items may be somewhat repetitive.

Point 5: Improve constantly and forever the system of production and service, to improve quality and productivity, and thus constantly decrease costs.

In the jargon of this book, get the system in-statistical-control by permanently or temporarily analyzing a control chart. If the output is not quantifiable or categorical to enable the use of an SPC chart, use your common sense. In any event, extraordinary occurrences must be flagged, categorized, Pareto-ized, and fixed. Then, and only then, interdepartmental teams must be formally established to begin solving the system problems. If it eventually seems that the troublesome system problems are all gone, use the teams to stamp out any further variability. This may be product physical variability, service time variability, or any other source of uncertainty. Variability is the root of all evil! We must, however, be patient enough to not treat system common causes as local faults in our quest to stamp out variability.

Quotas destroy the intangibles and the creative spirit required for continual improvement. In the United States, management seems to be mostly interested in just rewarding heroes. The solid citizens often go unnoticed. Consequently, we all become "hero-hopefuls." We are only interested in doing what gets us noticed (by the boss). Teamwork or compensating for others' weaknesses usually cannot be quantified in the short term. Everybody wants to "hit the home run." Even though four singles is a run, management often has few "attaboys" for single hits. The largest contrast with our culture that most U.S. executives report after working with Japanese firms is their fanatical interest in a continual stream of subtle product and process improvements. The type that singly do not draw much attention in the United States. Over time, however, "many drops yield a bucketful!" The bucket has remained empty for most by-the-numbers U.S. firms. This "drop at a time" is what Deming calls continual improvement. It only comes from teamwork and/or creative employees, with no lack of intangibles.

Point 8: Drive out fear.

There is no teamwork with fear. There are no lasting improvements to system problems with fear. The pie is smaller. It is every person for himself or herself as they struggle for a piece. They must struggle; it is a small pie. The pie can be bigger. I believe that overt, somewhat authoritative action must be taken by upper management to start the removal of fear. The managers must be told in no uncertain terms that it is not going to be tolerated. The removal of management by-the-numbers will make this an "easier pill to take." The removal of quantifiable objectives that are beyond the natural capabilities of the system will remove a considerable amount of fear. Publicly dismantle the power base of a few infamous General Patton types around the firm. The word will get around.

Point 9: Break down barriers between departments.

The interdepartmental teams are the most powerful tool for this. Breaking down the departmental barriers is a much needed spinoff of interdepartmental teams. It takes several years to see the total benefit. There may be noticeable improvements in five to six months, however.

Removal of MBO, quotas, or management by-the-numbers in general, will be a major tool in helping reduce the departmentalization. Inconsistent numerical goals, tradeoffs, etc., will be gone, and people will eventually work together better. It is impossible to give everyone quantifiable objectives that do not clash.

The business school systems experts started the organization-chart practice that puts everyone in a closed box and started much of this myopic departmental vision. Destroy the organizational chart and flaunt this practice. If you need an organizational chart to operate, you need to reorganize. Consider the case of one vice president who burned the organization chart in a meeting. No one ever forgot!

Cross-training and interdepartmental projects for employees help tremendously. Require all newly hired professionals to work in all departments for a considerable period before being permanently assigned. This practice is much more prevalent in Japan than in America.

Point 10: Eliminate slogans, exhortations, and zero defects propaganda.

They say you do not preach to the choir nor to the coffin. If I have not clearly made this point yet, you are in the coffin!

Point 11: Eliminate work standards (quotas). Substitute leadership. Eliminate MBO.

There will be additional comments on leadership in the next chapter. I do not, however, believe that many of the experts know yet what a good leader of the future should do, because we have few (or perhaps no) models of situations totally void of the Deadly Diseases. However, in the few situations I have seen of a near void of the Deadly Diseases, it seemed that the supervisors had to do practically nothing to point the people in the right direction. Management by-the-numbers does not have to be replaced with anything. People will begin to blossom if we get into the trenches with them.

Point 12: Remove barriers that rob the workers of pride of workmanship.

Pertaining to barriers to pride of workmanship, if the workers say the quality is not good enough to be sold to the customer, it is not to be shipped. Ever! Set up a fail-safe system to make this happen. In the absence of quotas, it will work. More on this point comes in the next chapter on performance appraisals. In the most straightforward case of manufacturing, numerical quotas quite frequently rid the production operators of their capability to "see the product," to quote a recent disheartened machine tender. They eventually lose their valued pride of workmanship. They seek employment elsewhere! Most of us want to feel that we are doing quality work. Forego no opportunity to enhance pride of workmanship.

Point 13: Institute a rigorous program of education and self-improvement.

As you will see later, Point 6 also pertains to training, but as it is applicable to new hires. Point 13 here mostly applies to the existing employees. Over the last 10 years, many American firms have made tremendous gains in this respect, but we are still deficient. Contrary to popular belief, the United States spends far more per pupil on elementary and secondary education than Japan or Germany. U.S. firms, however, spend less than the international competition for OJT and apprenticeship programs. No statistical data could be found to correlate corporate profitability with training expenditures, so you will have to trust a general observation of the author's covering a decade of consulting with about 100 clients and across many industries. It is not surprising that consultants work with many troubled firms, but it surprises many people that they work with even more extremely successful firms who cannot wait to get better. Consultants see few average firms.

Now to the training issue. It is as clear as the nose on your face when visiting many firms at the two extremes that the most profitable firms spend several times the average per employee on training, and are very careful to get their money's worth. Specific job skills are very important to them, but not necessarily more so than generalized, broadening training similar to the problem-solving tools on pages 31 through 42. If your regular employees are not in retraining (not initial basic skills classes) at least 10 days per year, you are behind the times. Some firms are setting the standards for us all; Motorola spends $40 million per year on training.

Around 1984 when the Deming message became popular, Point 13 received the most immediate attention. However, in many cases hundreds of thousands of dollars were expended on SPC and related training before there was a statistical vision by management. In fact, this is still happening! Education is said to be one of the few inputs to the productive process that is not subject to diminishing returns. This is generally true, with the exception of statistical training. Too much, too quick, with no vision and road map for implementation can be disheartening. In general, when the superiors got interested in the transition, management teams quickly rallied, threw money at the problem, created an image of "doing something" that the corporate observers could see; but very few improvements resulted. Why? All the efforts should have been through upper management's overt examples of ridding the corporation of the Deadly Diseases. The statistical training should be targeted, provided by a statistical master with a bit of knowledge of your system, and constantly directed toward the vision of eliminating the Deadly Diseases. Upper management is there, takes part, provides testimonials, and creates the first useable examples. They do not run out to catch a plane after the training sessions begin! The overt message is clear: "Follow me as I lead you," versus the near benign, "You have my support." Upper managers, if you think undirected generic statistical or management training will enable your employees to run your job for you, you are likely to become disappointed. I am afraid you have "to be there," in the beginning, in the middle, and in the end!

There is no turnkey statistical training plan that fits all cases, so I will not make the mistake of providing one. As a beginning to their statistical training, it is obvious that all managers must be exposed to the material in this book, with examples from their jobs. The engineering, quality department, and several internal gurus (to be) must carefully review and absorb the statistical literature as reported by Fellers. In about 98 percent of the cases, an experienced statistical master must help you get started. There are too many pitfalls that can totally discredit a novice before he learns the job of being a statistical advisor. At times a large customer will provide free consulting if you have become their sole source vendor partner. Some university professors are useful. Be suspect of this college group, however, until they pass your oral test on the Deming philosophy. Most PhD granting university departments of statistics do not even cover SPC. I think there are zero universities that have courses in the Deming vision taught to statistics majors. (This will change soon!) They do not know what it is! There are many credible consulting statisticians, however. They became streetwise after leaving school.

Point 13 also pertains to other types of training. In every case, no one employee in a department has all the "pieces of the puzzle." The "pieces" are scattered across the employees on different shifts and at various locations. Formal, coordinated training can help here; or if you want to see some real magic (synergy), get all the players to teach each other all they know through brainstorming sessions, etc.

The author has seen 20 percent improvements in quality and 10 percent increases in productivity just from this undertaking. The cost? Almost zero! No gadgets. No new computer systems. The typical office and factory worker in this country is expected to perform magic. They have never had the opportunity to be involved in coordinated, exhaustive training on their jobs. They have been "thrown to the wolves" to glean a few facts through OJT or whatever. Surprised? Ask around, you will see! They are afraid to ask questions once they are perceived to know the ropes. Hence, they learn mostly from their mistakes!

There are certainly other facets to this training issue; however, no comments are provided here because the author's only experience has been in statistical and quality management training and through an observation of the lack of basic training in most firms. Unless you know you are an industry leader in job training because you have taken many explicit steps to be where you are, you probably have problems.

Now a few obstacles are discussed that you will encounter while you are trying to eliminate the by-the-numbers disease. It is helpful to have identified these in advance and to have a plan for eliminating the Obstacles or a convincing discussion ready-made for the people in your organization who love to be the ones who always "shoot down" good suggestions. Don't let them catch you off guard because you have not done your homework. At times people will be grasping at straws while trying to defend their old antiquated ways. People do not mind change, but they despise being changed. They perceive you as trying to change them.

Obstacle 1: Hope for instant pudding.

The days of appropriately applying the quick fix are gone. You cannot install knowledge! Many of the existing problems are system issues requiring lengthy interdepartmental teams. If management only knows how to motivate heroes, most everyone will "try to take the hill by brute force like John Wayne" versus truly trying to get at the root causes. Most existing problems are people problems, and as managers, we generally will try to avoid addressing such issues. There are many reasons for this. One may be our bad experiences from the past. When we have been judgmental, based on the numbers, it has generally backfired, either directly or through passive resistance. Consequently, now we look for the clean and risk-free quick fix, the bureaucratic system, to get the job accomplished. If there were no Deadly Diseases, however, most people would eventually start to act like caring family members and we would need fewer systems. It will take a year or so for the corporate players to forgive us and for us to make believers out of them by example.

Have upper management in your firm explain to all levels of management that "there seems to be very little instant pudding left here. We are looking for permanent solutions to our system problems." Removal of the Deadly Diseases will make this statement a possible reality. The knee-jerk response from our treating system problems as local faults has made "gamblers or gunslingers" out of some of our potentially most competent employees. They do not have the energy or time to work with interdepartmental teams. It's instant pudding that interests them to solve their problems, or nothing at all, usually the latter. How do you change these people? Slowly, by example, by removing the Deadly Diseases from your management style, by being there, by paying attention, by coaching and nurturing, and occasionally only through retirement or death. (Natural causes only, please!)

Once upper management makes sure that the instant pudding analogy makes it down through all levels of management, a cultural change will be started such that the thought, "instant pudding," will provoke a negative psychological response.

Obstacle 2: The gadget mentality.

Many members of the work force are almost like zombies after years of being held accountable for seemingly insurmountable system problems. Consequently, and in manufacturing especially, everyone is too busy seeking the next physical gadget to solve their problems. Young engineers and MBAs are particularly guilty of this. They have superior technical skills and often premature responsibility to make things happen; however, previous generations of management have drained the work force of the intangibles and creative spirit. Consequently, the young professionals' earlier, first attempts to get employee cooperation failed, so they are hesitant to try again.

Gadgets can at times solve problems, and there is pressure to spend appropriated capital dollars; however, an application of statistics through interdepartmental teams can provide free solutions to chronic system problems, and these will be beyond most managers' wildest dreams. The team approach can break down some of the departmental barriers that have been preventing the synergy needed to solve system problems. Another system or gadget to compensate for those things that are "falling through the cracks" in your bureaucratic organization may not be necessary if you can break down some organizational barriers. Never approve an expenditure for another gadget except through a carefully constructed list of priorities from an interdepartmental team! Your needed cultural change will be set into motion when your subordinates get this message. And furthermore, the operative and front-line employees are already frequently disgusted with the firm for (in their minds) throwing more money away on useless gadgets when the basic problems (usually Deadly Diseases) still exist.

Learn to praise teams and groups for nongadget successes. Disproportionate praise or raises to the latest hero-apparent who was the loudest "squeaking wheel" or who achieved the most recent "flash in the pan" success will set back your effort by years as you try to change to a team culture. Some of your best people, whose successes this year were not of the noticeable type, will seek employment elsewhere. They do not tell you in exit interviews. We are taught not to burn our bridges.

Obstacle 3: Search for examples.

The Deadly Diseases are the same everywhere, and an expert with experience at other firms can help you. Do not, however, try to find a turnkey example from another firm to copy. Use statistical vision and common sense to cure your own Deadly Diseases.

Obstacle 4: Our problems are different.

The Deadly Diseases are the same everywhere, even though your firm may not be inflicted with all five of them. The exact scenario for making the transition, however, is different everywhere.

Obstacle 5: Poor teaching of statistical methods in industry.

Most of the credible teachers of the Deming statistical vision are consultants who have admirably "walked lightly" here because they did not want to look greedy or self-serving. So it is about time you heard the truth. It takes a master to teach the statistical vision to managers, especially beginners. He or she must have many years of experience in a large number of firms, advanced degrees in statistics, hands-on experience, a near-perfect bedside manner, and no fear. These people are in very short supply. Call one to check on his or her daily rates and you will see!

Attendance at seminars is sometimes good, but never complete. Someone with no local routine or administrative duties and with no political or bureaucratic concerns will be needed on site to get you started on the transition. It is difficult for the internal employees to accept an insider as having the amount of insight and power wielded by a statistical guru. Generally, the results from the first interdepartmental team pay the consulting fee several times over.

An exception: A well-trained insider can train production and clerical operators to appreciate and use simple SPC charts. It takes more skill and communicative ability to do even this than most firms think, however. Do not designate the local misfit as statistical coordinator. Use one of your most valued employees who is the most difficult to be removed from other assignments.

Obstacle 6: Our problems are with the work force.

This is almost never true. The problem is with management. The knee-jerk reactions, conflicting numerical objectives, loss of intangibles, and bureaucratic suboptimization are silently killing the firm. The workers are doing their best within the system. Mingle around in the trenches. Find several dozen examples of how the situation looks like employee laziness, but at a deeper level is actually a system problem that can be corrected only by management. Expound on these examples to shut up colleagues who state Obstacle 6. A classic example was the case of secretarial errors. It looked like the secretary was careless and indifferent. An interdepartmental team discovered that the main problems were:

- Telephone interruptions and the need for answering machines.
- Copy machine traffic.
- Sexual innuendos by several co-workers.
- Poor planning by requestors.
- Ergonomics issues.

Obstacle 7: False starts.

The statistical vision should be complete in at least one level of management above and below the strata presently of interest. Your beginnings must be carefully guided by a master. The first attempts must be successful. Be patient!

Obstacle 8: The fallacy of zero defects.

An in-control system can produce defect problems. The system must be altered by management to prevent defects "upstream." You cannot jawbone employees into "doing better" and have it last. It takes management action. If in-control, the same system produces the good and bad product or service. You cannot eliminate system problems by edict or jawboning.

Obstacle 9: Anyone who can help us must understand all about our business.

There are many misconceptions here. Many firms have misinterpreted Deming here and gone too far in the other direction. For sure, the guru does not have to be a veteran in your industry. However, it is difficult for your people to accept the message of seminars by outsiders who have no knowledge of your processes, system, or product. If you plan to acquire outside help from a guru, you

probably should buy some days of his or her time to initially train
him or her. The types of credible people to coach you can absorb facts
like a sponge and operate like a veteran after only several days of
tutoring by you.

*Obstacle 10: Too heavy an emphasis on NPV, internal rate of
return (IRR), ROI, payback, or other quantitative capital budgeting tools when assessing the desirability of quality or customer
service enhancing requests for funds.*

The quantitative capital budgeting tools may at times be
acceptable, but never when the expenditure will enhance product
quality, customer service, or employee pride of workmanship. These
returns are generally unquantifiable; and in all cases the true future
income flows are five to 10 times what anyone could ever predict. The
unknowns such as value of a satisfied customer or future worth of a
fulfilled worker are more profitable than you could ever dream of.
The financial wizards do not understand this. Create a special book-
keeping code for capital requests that affect quality, customer service,
or employee pride of workmanship. Train the people pertaining to
what this code means. Then see that the coded requests get special
attention. Only the top, visionary managers can disapprove of these
coded requests for funds. With the dampening of the NPV, ROI, or
IRR system, little will actually change for insightful organizations.
There must be constant pressure by management to keep expenditures in line. In other words, we must pay attention. By-the-numbers
systems (NPV, ROI, or IRR) never relaxed this need to be alert. They
only made life difficult for employees who were trying to continually
improve quality, customer service, or pride of workmanship (the big
three). In most organizations this type of pressure has worn down
most of the solid citizens.

Many executives say that they have no MBO, and that their
firms do not practice by-the-numbers management. There are probably a few cases of an absolute void of numbers management, but very
few. If you look closely, you will generally find secret islands of
by-the-numbers management. Often enough to thwart the creative
spirit of the entire firm through the "weakest link in the chain"

phenomenon. For this reason upper management must be authoritative to cure this Deadly Disease. Counseling and follow-up are required. Every six months or so, ask the lowest level employees if numerical quotas are still the norm. They will generally tell you.

Many accountants and financial experts have gotten defensive toward the Deming proponents. This was an unnecessary breakdown in communications. No one has any complaints about tallying business results, or the standard accounting practices for achieving the bottom-line numbers or indicators of business performance. We all need an eventual report card for the long term. It is the use of these numbers in a short-term, nonstatistical, unvisionary fashion that is bad, especially when judging or trying to motivate people.

The Deadly Disease of the next chapter is the formal, by-the-numbers performance appraisal. The required statistical vision is very similar to this chapter. Management by-the-numbers was chosen by the author as the first Deadly Disease to be discussed because its statistical message is so strong. A good implementation starting point, however, may be Deadly Disease 2 pertaining to performance appraisal. Usually the performance appraisal system is created by people in the top echelons and is thus easily dismantled only by visionary upper managers.

A big thrust lately is to empower the hourly workers to use their knowledge to help the company become more profitable. There is much merit to this trend. Generally the rank and file have answers to many of the firm's biggest problems. If someone in the firm would (or could) just ask them, millions of dollars could be saved by not buying gadgets or by not initiating unnecessary management control schemes. (How do you think we consultants get most of our recommendations? From the rank and file!) On numerous occasions when asked, "Why haven't you told someone before?" the front-line employees always replied with comments such as:

"No one ever asked me."

"I told the supervisor once, and he did not take action."

"They would never listen."

"Some engineer will steal the credit."

"I am not paid to think."

Why is first-line supervision resisting this obvious trend toward participative management down to the lowest levels? There seem to be several contributing factors, such as the supervisor's fear of becoming unnecessary and losing his or her job, the supervisor's dislike of management usurping his or her authority, or the supervisor's fondness for giving orders and being the boss.

However, an almost universal situation that exists when there is very strong resistance by the first-line supervisors to participative management is the presence of by-the-numbers quotas to be met (either officially or implied). When you get to the root causes of the supervisory resistance, it is easy to understand why they do not want to give up control when it is they who are personally responsible for the "numbers." They have suffered with the numbers game for years, and now things seem to be getting worse as they are seemingly losing control.

Is there ever a case where strict motivation solely by-the-numbers in a business is the most appropriate managerial practice? Of course there is, when all the following conditions exist:

1. You do not care about this person.
2. The business situation is immune from the knee-jerk response.
3. You do not care if this person remains here.
4. There is no need for the worker to be creative.
5. The worker has no power to ruin the image of the firm.
6. This employee can never advance beyond this job.
7. There is no opportunity to improve costs or quality in his or her work area.
8. You have ultimate authority and power over his or her work life. And you like it this way.
9. There are no developing young managers watching you whose futures you may badly impact by setting a bad example.
10. The world is going to end tomorrow; there is no future.

11. There is absolutely no need for this person to interact with his or her associates through teamwork to improve profitability.

If there is such a situation, it may be the chain gang or something similar. Shoveling coal into a furnace when it takes two tons per hour to heat the building may be such a case, but probably not! Now, do you get the message?

There must be goals and objectives, but only qualitative and process-oriented ones. Not only will this new emphasis prevent many knee-jerk reactions and burnout resulting in a loss of creativity, it also forces the manager to learn the process well enough to make his required contribution in the upcoming system changes. If you feel that you must, in the interest of time management, espouse wishful numerical goals to "get these issues off my desk," you simply do not have time to do your job.

5

PERFORMANCE APPRAISAL BY-THE-NUMBERS DEADLY DISEASE 2

I make many visits to business firms to offer consulting advice and to conduct training sessions. Over the last decade this has happened about a thousand times — literally. With an accuracy of over 99 percent, within 10 minutes of the arrival at a facility it is obvious if the infamous performance appraisal cycle occurred recently: The receptionist for the first time is either rude or has the appearance of an injured puppy. My plant escort is usually solemn, versus his or her normal cheery demeanor. The organization members who I already know and trust corner me in private to see if any of my other clients need their services. "The grass must be greener somewhere else," they say. No one seems receptive to new ideas; my visit for the day to make suggestions is wasted. People are not even friendly toward each other. Everyone is quietly sulking at his or her desk as a "lone wolf." The important unknowns and unknowables, which are usually in no one's job description, are purposely of no interest to anyone. They are sticking to measurables, the noticeable that will make the next performance appraisal cycle less disturbing. There is no teamwork. It is "every person for himself or herself."

These negative feelings are strong for about four weeks, but remain to some extent all year.

This scenario is not an isolated event. It is everywhere. For whatever good reasons there may be for numerically based performance appraisal systems the way it is typically accomplished (I have found none whatsoever), the pain and suffering discussed above is more than enough to lead visionary people to discontinue the system as currently practiced. It is killing the team spirit, causing over half your employee turnover, and ruining good people's lives. The impact on the profitability of your firm is difficult to quantify; however, the author estimates a 20 percent reduction in bottom-line profits. Everyone in the organization can do his or her work exactly as prescribed in the job description, and the firm can still fail miserably. The truly important contributions of employees are the results of actions that enhance teamwork, that break down departmental barriers, that enhance trust, that improve the unknowns and unknowables, that teach colleagues how to perform more effectively, ad infinitum. The measurables inherently get considerable attention, as they should. But the unmeasurables are at least 10 times more important. In other words, those things that cannot be quantified are deemphasized by your performance appraisal system. And the intangibles are lost.

Before the statistical vision is reviewed in the context of the evils of by-the-numbers performance appraisal, let's clarify one point that has confused many transition-hopefuls. Some sort of performance appraisal is a necessary part of management. In fact, the typical employee needs even more feedback. It is the way we do it that ruins organizational performance and makes about half of the players think that we may be Antichrists in suits. As you will see shortly, performance appraisal should be informal and frequent. A performance appraisal system and the often accompanying MBO controls should not be used as an attempt to get people to simply do their jobs. Job descriptions, informal communications, and common sense are what accomplish this. If there are to be stated yearly objectives, they should encompass extraordinary desires or special opportunities. In other words, goal setting should entail the excitement of unique challenges. Once a firm starts the Deming transition, the enhanced teamwork, reduced stress, and improved cross-functional cooperation will begin to motivate employees to highlight these opportunities. By all means there should be no numbers of any sort; no rankings, no strata, no percentiles, and no forced blank spaces that *must* be filled in pertaining to recommendations for improvement.

Good managers are coaches, not judges. Sure all people can improve; however, the judgmental by-the-numbers formal performance appraisal simply does not make this happen. Instead, it draws weird negative responses. The downside far exceeds any possible upside of performance appraisal as generally practiced now. The main thrust of this chapter is to get you to discontinue what you are doing, as it pertains to performance appraisal. In many not so extreme cases, it would be acceptable to have no formal system whatsoever. For the more bureaucratic firms where the "so-called" managers in charge cannot be sure that direct supervisors are coaching and constructively providing feedback to their people, a few recommendations for the new formal performance appraisal will be stated later in this chapter. Based on the present way of accomplishing formal performance appraisal in most firms, it seems to upper management that the raters in the lower echelons would be able to provide constructive, tactful feedback that would be helpful to the employees. But this happens less than one time in a hundred. Practically no one has the empathy, charisma, or whatever else it takes to perform this judgmental job. The person being rated generally feels defensive, crushed, and eager to go elsewhere to work. Teamwork is dead! Managers who are forced by the bureaucracy to perform this judgmental job tell the author that they hate doing it, but it has to be done. Why? For no reason, as you will see shortly. Almost no one likes the system. Let's stop it, now! Send a copy of this book to your company president with this chapter highlighted.

Now to the statistical vision. If we had many years of accurate data and a close association with all employees, and if we had statistical wisdom, evaluating people with statistical help by-the-numbers could work. It would, however, take no less than five years of accurate performance data on all players and the advice of a master statistician all through the years to make this happen. This situation never exists.

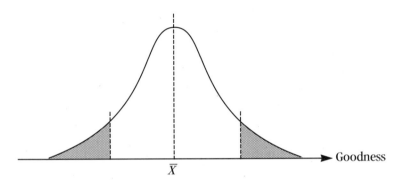

Figure 5.1   Statistical Distribution for Any Group

And as you will see, pertaining to what to do for the really important issues such as dismissal, reassignment, or promotions for extreme employees, you know by gut feel without the results of a performance appraisal system. YOU KNOW, YOU KNOW, YOU KNOW! Some say that the performance appraisal system is in place for the non-extreme (good or bad) employees; however, as you will see, these are the solid citizens for which most systems do not work. Consider Figure 5.1 as a philosophical example. With an overall measure of goodness on the horizontal axis, for any group of people, half are below the system average ($\overline{X}$), by definition, and about 1 to 5 percent are in the shaded extreme areas.

The people at the two extremes are called outliers by statisticians. (We use weird names for obvious things so that you have to hire us to help you!) These outlier people are statistically out-of-control (good or bad), and you cannot help but already know who they are. They stand out. You know; everyone knows! You do not need numbers, forced rankings, or percentiles to justify highly rewarding the high-side outliers or helping the low-side outliers. Do you fire the low-siders? Preferably not. Possible options:

- Check to see if their OJT was poor.
- Check to see if they have physical limitations.
- Check to see if there are supervisory personality conflicts.
- Check to see if there are environmental disruptions.
- Check to see if there is a lesser job available.

If the answer to all these questions is "no," try to bear the cost of relocating the low-siders to another job. Placing them in a job for which they were unsuited, or selecting them in the first place, was a management failing. If all fails, give them two months' pay and escort them to their cars — be sympathetic and nice. Some large firms, however, have managed not to fire anyone for many years, so apparently it is possible! For a small group of less than 100 employees, there may be no outliers at all. Philosophically, as the curve for the entire group shifts far enough to the right, there will eventually be no low-side outliers to be dealt with.

Now back to the team players represented by the unshaded portion of the curve of Figure 5.1. This is the group that has been devastated by the performance appraisal system, as presently practiced. Obviously, they are not all equal pertaining to corporate contribution, but there is far too much statistical risk for you to categorize or rank these solid citizens. System common cause variability generally dwarfs any small differences among solid citizens. The gains that you may make by trying to positively reward the slightly above average people or by constructively criticizing those apparently a bit below average are far outweighed by all the negative responses elicited by the mistakes of ranking of mid-range people. This is assuming you do not have any rater bias or honestly make any judgmental mistakes. Another important issue is the total inability of the solid citizens to enhance teamwork after the performance appraisal ranking has destroyed their morale. There is no synergy. The bureaucracy goes on, but the pie is so small that even the high-side outliers' large slice is smaller than an average piece of the larger "pie" that could result if teamwork existed. You cannot even begin to imagine how great the corporate performance could be if there were good teamwork where members took it upon themselves to know of and to compensate for the weaknesses of their colleagues. Many managers have expressed to the author that our players work as a team, and a few do a fair job. However, few executives can even imagine what real teamwork would be like. There are no role models. "Teamwork" to the typical executive means "we do not openly fight," which is good, but not enough. The author has seen precious few cases of real teamwork. The type noticed in a professional orchestra. (Read on. I am about to describe your boss!)

Half of any group of people are below the average, by definition. Why tell them? Most of them are performing many "bass clef" functions while the fast-burners are being noticed playing "treble clef." How does this sound to you coming from your boss?

YOU ARE BELOW AVERAGE!
YOU ARE BELOW AVERAGE!
YOU ARE BELOW AVERAGE!

Below average may be very good! Half of us are there. Half of the astronauts, half of the Nobel Prize recipients, half of the priests, half the Olympic athletes, half of the San Francisco 49ers, and probably you, too! (Fifty percent chance.) In any event, why break a person's will by telling them? Work out an action plan to nurture and coach them through continual improvement. If we are allowed to work as a team instead of "every person for himself or herself," and if we all continually improve, the firm will be world class. The "pie" will be very big! Most of the plus-or-minus variability about the average in the unshaded portion of Figure 5.1 is within the system. As discussed earlier, only with teamwork through interdepartmental teams can this variability be diminished. Only upper management can effectively respond to the system recommendations made by the teams.

Pertaining to these solid citizens, Michael Beer of the Harvard Business School made an accurate statement when he said, "Total performance is a complex collage of competence, skills, and knowledge. Most people are in the middle. All we need to do is to identify the really outstanding performers and the (truly) poor ones."[26] Even when some employees see the performance appraisal system in the most positive way, that is documented positive reinforcement by the boss, we have still lost elsewhere among the other workers a thousand times more than we have gained! We have lost teamwork of the masses which is our only hope of breaking down the organizational barriers that will improve the unknowns and unknowables to make us world class. In the minds of all the hero-hopefuls, they harbor the thought that "if you are not seen doing it alone, you do not get credit for it." It is not what you do that counts, but what it is perceived that you do. The result:

TEAMWORK IS DEAD!

What is left are fragmented and isolated spurts of stroke-eliciting behaviors, sometimes canceling each other out, often causing other knee-jerk responses, and always preventing the solving of long-term system problems. Everyone, even the apparent winners, are flustered, confused, and frustrated in the end. You see burned-out, ugly facial expressions on the employees as they leave the facility at the end of the day.

To make matters even worse, numerical objectives by which employees are judged at the end of the year are often treated in an attribute fashion. To a statistician, the word "attribute" means a variable that has only two levels: good/bad, on/off, yes/no, present/not present, objective met/objective not met, etc. An employee may continually improve in a variable like production or sales, but yet not meet the numerical quota (objective). However, at the end of the year he or she still receives the message:

YOU DID NOT MEET YOUR OBJECTIVES!
YOU DO NOT MEET STANDARDS!
YOU MUST DO BETTER!

The employee knows better. The employee knows of the presence of the system barriers. The employee is demoralized, and loses his or her creative spirit and desire to continually improve the system (the intangibles are gone). The employee looks for another job.

More on the statistical vision now follows. First look at the control chart on Figure 5.2. The philosophical variable plotted for a hypothetical employee is performance, whatever that is. The higher it is, the better.

Note that the typical employee over time does vary about his or her own average. There are no exceptions! We talk about doing our best. This is nonsense. We all have an average and considerable plus-or-minus variability. Obviously, however, we want to raise the former and reduce the latter. A "snapshot" sampling for an employee will

Performance

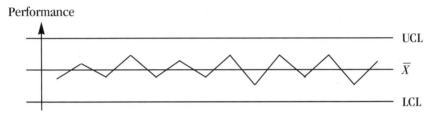

Figure 5.2   Performance Control Chart

almost always provide a mistake! Eventually, however, you know. You do not need a "system" for this. Consider the evils of rating people, especially by-the-numbers, by analyzing Figure 5.3.

The big bell-shaped curve is for the entire group at a point in time. The smaller internal curves are for Harry (H) and Sue (S) over time. Their common cause variabilities are depicted by the plus-or-minus limits of the small bell curves. Harry is obviously above the average ($\overline{X}$). Sue is below, but for brief periods, either may appear (or be) on the other side of the norm ($\overline{X}$). Quantification, or trying to nail down in the short term where each person is on this continuum, is far too risky. The cost of the mistakes far outweigh any possible gains. The people do not forgive you for mistakes! Forget the numbers! Let it be! (Good title for a song! Go listen to it. Lennon and McCartney knew this in 1969.) The improved total performance from enhanced teamwork will give us a bigger pie to split if we do not take the risk of ranking solid citizens. We all win! All players can possibly feel the creative spirit to continually improve. Then we have arrived. Will a few slightly higher than average people leave instead of patiently waiting to be noticed over the long term? I suppose a few will, but not nearly as many as you think. The "bigger pie" from teamwork and the perceived level of fairness will keep most committed team players around. The increased creativity and productivity of the heretofore unheralded solid citizens will far overshadow the exiting of a few "professional career managers." Are there other necessary ingredients for corporate success after the numerical performance appraisal is abolished? Of course there are, but we already have most of these other things. Accountants can count; engineers

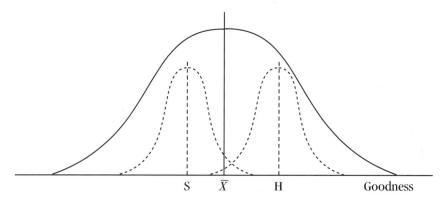

S $\overline{X}$ H   Goodness

Figure 5.3   You Cannot Quantify People!

can engineer; production people can produce; let them do it with pride and dignity! What they cannot do within most by-the-numbers organizations is work as a true team, to bring forth synergy with no private agendas.

People often leave the firm when the performance appraisal system demoralizes them. Some managers claim that this so-called natural turnover is part of the normal process and is needed to bring in "new blood." This is a poor managerial strategy. The company's Deadly Diseases demoralize and burn out the employees, we turn them loose as broken-down, mangled carcasses, then we bring in a new crop who will tolerate us for a few years while we unknowingly "wring the life out of them." The firm is then run by many new hires who cannot help but make frequent mistakes until they learn how to stay out of trouble by not making waves. We need a few waves. We need lifetime, committed employees. Company-specific knowledge shows no diminishing returns, and is free with senior employees if we do not burn them out. As you have to continually "go back to the well for water," it costs you more and more for salaries to get people to enter. The word gets around pertaining to how difficult it is to work at your company. Then the new hires make as much money as your senior family members. Then the experienced people who you need the most leave or become demoralized.

Many Americans pride themselves as rugged individualistic "gunslingers" who are not afraid to "get the cards out on the table." Maybe all those old westerns on television helped ruin us. I can see it vividly as I watched John Wayne as a child. While drinking straight liquor right out of the old bottle, he said something like, "If you don't like the situation, I'll shoot you and move on across the Mexican border." Perhaps this approach was acceptable around 1850, but not now. We need teamwork, not rugged heroes. We need nurturing and continual improvement; many droplets eventually fill the bucket. The interdepartmental, complex nature of the problems presently plaguing most firms cannot be solved by hero-hopeful gunslingers. Get them out of the mainstream. Coach them on working as team members. Only reward their performance as part of a team. They may catch on or they may decide to go ruin a competitor's culture.

Sometimes we fail to appreciate the vulnerability of humankind. You cannot tell solid citizens that they are below average and expect them to keep their spirit. It would seem that a "kick in the pants" would inspire them. Not likely! (Not even when you are correct in your assessment.) And there's probably about a 50 percent chance of system common cause leading you to error. (Not to mention rater bias!) One issue slowing the curing of the numerical performance appraisal Deadly Disease by top management pertains to the exceptional talents and motivation of most upper managers. They are, and always were, high-side outliers and always got the attention and rewards they deserved. They are not empathetic to the plight of the solid citizens who are hurt the most by numerically based performance appraisal systems. They never were solid citizens themselves.

Consider the case of a local hospital administrator who decided to get a local newspaper to provide monthly features this year on his 12 best doctors. This sounds good to a person of no statistical vision. But it stinks and does millions of dollars worth of unmeasurable damage to a group of very sensitive doctors. For reasons discussed earlier, how can you really tell who the best 12 are? What about the demoralization of the unchosen doctors? Assuming we did know who the best 12 were, what about person 13, 14, or 15? What are these people? Chopped liver? Absolutely not! These are truly exceptional performers whose feelings must be carefully protected. The negative feelings of the unchosen exceptional and solid citizen doctors far outweigh the positive impact on the chosen 12. How can you designate the chosen 12? (Employee of the month is the same.) Maybe use a roulette wheel with all present as witnesses? Seriously, if you must have 12 to discuss in the newspaper, a roulette wheel elicits no negative response. A statistically knowledgeable person realizes that life is really a roulette wheel anyway as long as the people around you have no statistical vision. Consider the case of the fast food restaurant manager who gives a reward to the crew who has the highest single daily sales for the month. In the long term, the crews (note the plural here) have a large impact on sales; however, on a day-to-day basis, deseasonalized sales are predominantly a random variable (roulette wheel). What should the restaurant manager do? Maybe nothing that fosters internal competition. Too much internal competition can lead to destructive behaviors; in fact, it usually will. Perhaps the restaurant manager can offer a group incentive for increases in total monthly sales. Perhaps he or she can start cross-crew brainstorming sessions to see if the total knowledge is greater than the fragmented sum of its parts. Maybe the manager can start an interdepartmental team to help identify system problems for the manager or the manager's boss to solve. In other words, pay close attention to the process of providing food service and forget about stirring up internal competition in the search for a method of managing without paying attention to the process. We want teamwork, synergy, and reductions in variability, not internal competition. Your competitors give you enough competition. We want creativity. The "voice of judgment," whether from within or from the boss, and our constant struggle to impress others destroys creativity. Being able to candidly contribute as a team member in a nonjudgmental environment can bring out heretofore untapped creativity. The absence of the fear of being judged can enable the development of concentration powers, efficiency, accuracy, and humor.

As a result of the performance appraisal, about 80 percent of the people at times feel betrayed, and for several reasons. One is the statistical risk just discussed, being unnecessarily told that YOU ARE BELOW AVERAGE! In addition, there are the obvious issues of supervisor bias, personality conflicts, rater differences across the firm, poor bedside manner of the boss, ignorance and incompetence of the supervisor, and at times, just plain stupidity. Only about one person in a thousand can give constructive criticism without destroying the person. Do not take this risk. You cannot train a person to do this either. Standardized, by-the-numbers performance appraisal or qualitative but judgmental systems always break down trust in the organization. This is unbelievably horrible. Many studies have shown that *the* number one ingredient of all great places to work is trust. Trust means there's no back-stabbing, no window dressing, no unfair treatment, and it's fun to work there. Do contented cows produce great milk? Not always, of course, but at least they are allowed to contribute and may do so. They do not seek greener pastures every several years. They stay where they are and become experienced.

An executive once stated that the comments about the demoralizing effects of performance appraisals were simply not true in his case. How could he have known? Were his people going to tell him that his "carrot and stick" approach did not work? They feared reprisal next time around! As Americans, we are supposed to be able to stand up and take it like a man! John Wayne did in many old movies. The fact is that few of us can take it, even if "it" is accurate, which it never is for all employees for the statistical reasons just discussed. The carrot does not motivate. The high-side outliers cannot help but be singled out with no formal system at all. They do not need the performance appraisal carrot. The stick has no good lasting effect either. The low-side outliers likely know it too, and you know it. The mid-ground solid citizens are too close together to call, even though the system often makes them look a bit different for short periods. Incorrectly giving the solid citizens the "carrot" is confusing. Incorrectly giving them the "stick" is demoralizing. What do they need?

- Training on the extended process.
- Road maps.

- Technical training.
- Training in problem-solving skills.
- Membership on interdepartmental teams.
- Nurturing.
- Coaching.
- A "piece of the pie" from a group bonus.
- Solitude at times.
- A closer association with the finished product (customers).

A survey of over 400 firms confirmed the fallacy of the formalized, by-the-numbers, judgmental performance appraisal. The general consensus was that they were inaccurate, inefficient, unnecessary, and embarrassing.[25] They focus on the end product, not the process that produces the desired result. Not having the slightest idea of what to do, and with the hope of getting these "people" issues off his or her desk, the superstitiously trained manager lays out the objectives along with the threat of negative consequences if you fail. Does this get any results? Occasionally temporary, unlasting, islands of short-term results, but with a tremendous human cost. In the long term, you have little when the negatives and the (unlikely, but possible) positives cancel out. The system drives out the intangibles, destroys creativity and teamwork, and causes constant turmoil as solid citizens resign and are replaced by new hires. Two-thirds of America's middle managers regard their bosses as inadequate! Why? Here are the reasons given[26]:

- Overcontroller
- Spotlighter
- Crisis-maker
- Underdelegator
- Stoic

Can you see how these survey findings correspond to the first two Deadly Diseases? Now we know why! Most of this lack of respect is from actually trying too hard with our infamous management systems such as MBO, performance appraisal, etc. Peter Drucker once said that most of what we do as managers prevents people from actually doing their jobs. After 20 years of thought, I finally understand what he meant. Management involves, (among other things):

- Being there.
- Setting examples.
- Statistical vision.
- Not demoralizing people.
- Technical competence.
- Coaching.
- Helping people.

And it involves many other qualities too numerous to mention. What we do not need are more systematic (systems) ways to inspire people. Systems do not work in this respect. The types of demoralizing systems that we now have to dismantle seemed to work between 1950 and 1970 because anything was successful at that time. There was little international competition. Our leaders became superstitiously trained believing they had created a profession of management. There is no such thing; now we know. Also, the increasing size of most firms during the 1950s and 1960s led to the need for universal, objective, apparently fair systems to be used corporate-wide (we thought!). If the organization is so big that it seems we need such systems, the bureaucracy must be diminished. Here are some ideas of Naisbitt and Aburdene for reducing bureaucracy:

1. Reverse performance appraisals.
2. Divisionalize and decentralize, whatever these mean.
3. Use first names only.
4. Keep minimal files and paperwork. Expect people to know what is going on, then there will be pressure to simplify.
5. Call all people "associates."
6. Use no organizational chart.
7. Use no executive dining rooms, parking, or restrooms (let them read the graffiti about management!).
8. Have machines or executives answer all phones.
9. Speak only to pleasant people.

It has been said that a bureaucrat is a person who operates in a fashion such that the smaller the issue, the more skillful they are at it. People issues are not small. They are big and cannot be relegated to a system created by the corporate technocrats. In one firm the CEO got a bit of the Deming vision and asked the corporate human relations group to make recommendations for a better performance appraisal system. It had always taken about six corporate human relations people to administer the present system. This work involved rewriting (but not likely improving) the system every three to four years, filing, logging, monitoring, processing grievances, and making upper management reports. According to the Deming vision, a good new system would require little of this work (as discussed later). Could you expect these people to recommend the discontinuance of their jobs? Of course not, and they did not. They created an equally bad new system. What should the CEO have done? First, ensure the human relations employees continued employment (otherwise he will forever be paying them to do useless work). Second, announce that the performance appraisal system, as we know it, is no longer to be used. Discontinued, in one fell swoop! This may take a frontal lobotomy for some uninformed diehards. Try training them. Then have a statistical visionary who is also a corporate solid citizen create a new form as discussed below. Note that the word system was not used. We do not need a system. In fact, maybe you need nothing at all pertaining to performance appraisal. If you are afraid to go cold turkey, consider the following recommendations:

1. In any event, provide expert statistical training so that superstitiously trained managers will not think you are crazy when everything begins to change.
2. Discontinue all numerical quotas to suppress the knee-jerk response.
3. Encourage frequent feedback through management training.

4. Once per year, hold three- to four-hour sessions on career guidance for all employees. No numbers, no rankings, no percentiles, no required negative judgments, and little documentation other than what is needed to make sure that this is happening.

5. On a case-by-case basis, if a supervisor cannot subjectively counsel in a nonjudgmental fashion, do not make him or her do it. Let the next level of management do it, or find the judgmental supervisor a new job. (Try the competition first!)

6. Base pay on market values for skill, a seniority formula, and the overall health of the firm. If there are many market-value discrepancies, there must be an even adjustment of all relevant employees based on some kind of seniority and percentage below market formula. The high- and low-side outliers do not apply here. These people deserve extreme treatment. There are not enough of these guys to significantly affect the formula.

7. If there is a bonus system, make it the same percentage for everyone. Teamwork is what you are missing. Presently, you likely have suboptimization and a resulting smaller pie.

8. Assume that the entire work force needs the broadened training of the entire operation and the extended process, to include vendors and customers. Provide this training.

9. It is obvious who should be promoted. Base promotions on ability to enhance teamwork, special assignments, assessment centers, and customers' remarks. A master of the Deming statistical vision must be involved in promotion decisions.

10. Immediately start developing employees to replace managers who will eventually retire. Don't let superstitiously trained diehards be your only alternatives.

11. Never cut anyone's pay. Let inflation do this if it is a must.

12. Except for high- or low-side outliers (2 to 5 percent), cost

of living raises are the same for everyone. Too fine of a division for people is often in error. Item 6 takes care of market values. This is a hard "pill" for non-visionary managers to take. Train them first. Some will leave the firm. Good riddance!

13. There is "no grease for squeaking wheels," pertaining to raises or promotions. If this is your only organizational knowledge, get back into the trenches. You are presently in deep trouble from lack of process knowledge.

14. Consider supervisory training in behavior modification (where applicable), Maslow's hierarchy of needs, Herzberg's two factor theory, coaching, SPC, and the Deming philosophy. The trainer must be a master with process knowledge.

15. Improve the selection process. Correlate current performance with historical data.

16. Assess managers mostly on six issues:
    Knowledge and use of the Deming philosophy.
    Enhancing of teamwork.
    The nurturing and coaching of employees.
    Removal of barriers to pride of workmanship.
    Reducing the number of vendors (see Chapter 8).
    Improving training relating to issue 8.
    Reduction of process and product variability.

Do numerical goals such as sales, production, or price-to-earnings (P/E) ratio no longer matter? Of course they still do! Team players and our bigger is better national culture will get these for you with little pressure. Obviously, your firm is doing many of the right things and could identify a few more. Elimination of the old performance evaluation system will be "cheered by the masses," but a few outspoken managers of "the old school" will sense a void. The 16 items will help fill this void. This change of heart will take two to three years for most of the diehards, retirement for some, a "bullet" for others!

Many firms are silently curing this performance appraisal Deadly Disease. Others are talking about it. Here are some examples.

At Ford, they greatly reduced the number of categories in which people were to be placed. In the old days, you were always told:

YOU ARE BELOW AVERAGE!
YOU ARE IN THE BOTTOM 25 PERCENT.
YOU ARE IN THE MIDDLE 25 PERCENT.
YOU ARE IN THE UPPER 10 PERCENT.
(I could stand hearing this, I suppose!)

Now with the new system all the solid citizens are assumed within the system and not placed in a percentile or strata, as before. The outliers are restricted to only a few percent. These extraordinary cases are dealt with as before. There also were several other qualitative changes to the Ford system not discussed here. A subsequent confidential survey of 2,000 participants yielded a high 79 percent approval of the new system over the old.[27] The Ford survey was performed only one year after the implementation of the new plan. It takes longer than one year to get total buy in. Three years later the acceptance of the new method would likely have well exceeded the already high 79 percent. There would never be 100 percent acceptance. About 15 percent of the managers in any organization have been torn down by the system to the point of never cooperating in anything new.

General Motors was not to be outdone by Ford. Three years later, they scrapped their old performance appraisal system which arbitrarily gave 10 percent of the staff a poor rating and 50 percent a below average ranking. Now 5 percent get a star rating, the high-side outliers, and 95 percent get no ranking at all. Corporate insiders now attribute the resulting enhanced teamwork as a large part of the success of the new Quad 4 engine, as an example. As reported by Meon, now for a change, all departments work together completely as a team.

After grasping the Deming vision at Temple-Inland Forest Products, Evadale, Texas, the by-the-numbers performance appraisal was dismantled in one fell swoop. When this announcement was made at a meeting of all managers, there was a loud applause by the attendees. Like all management teams, they were ready to eliminate this Deadly Disease. The new system of objective setting and feedback looked more like item 16 in the previous list. (Thanks to W. C. Cole and David Ashcraft of Temple-Inland for this insightful example.)

Many middle and lower-tier managers are subjected to the tyranny of nonvisionary corporate technocrats who force them to do ridiculous performance appraisals. The effective ones diffuse the situation in some way. "I believe my boss just fills them in and passes them up the line. We never see them, but she is made to do it. (I hope I did not get you into trouble, boss.)" Upper managers should stop all this wasted effort by assuring the corporate technocrats of suitable employment doing something else, versus processing useless or harmful performance appraisals.

A student in an MBA class stated that his organization had to do formal by-the-numbers performance appraisals to short circuit the good ole boy network and to look out for minorities. Let me tell you, it does neither. If there is enough basically wrong with your people for this type of thing to be worrisome, some people will figure out a way to beat the system. Surgically solve the basic problem. The cancers must be removed and publicly disgraced! The human relations experts tell me that the elaborate numerical performance evaluations are often necessary when it comes to employee dismissal. They say that if in court, only if you can say, "This guy is a 5.2 and the average is 5.6," you can justify dismissal. This simply is not so! Ask a lawyer who is not earning his or her livelihood by defending your numerical performance appraisal system. To build a case against an unworthy employee, create a file on issues such as number of days absent, days late, and specific qualitative occurrences witnessed by other trustworthy employees.

Here are some of Deming's 14 Points that help you rid yourself of the performance appraisal system. Many of the discussions have already been provided and will not be repeated here.

Point 1: Create constancy of purpose to improve product and quality to stay in business and to provide jobs.

This is a multifaceted point that shows up in several places in this book. As it pertains to performance appraisal, the message is to take measures to keep the list of corporate players constant. Do not drive them away with arbitrary (truly or seemingly) performance appraisal systems. We need experienced, visionary people. Turnover is bad, but fire the horrible bad guys who are willing to make people suffer to enhance their careers! Do not patiently try to discourage them to leave by unfair treatment. The side effects often touch others.

Point 6: Institute training on the job.

This point is mostly for new hires. There must be a formal training program that teaches them the corporate mission (discussed later), the theoretical aspects of the job, the extended process, and the how to. OJT is only a small part of this process. OJT as a sole training tool is a despicable American practice that is greatly contributing to our trade deficit. Do not let the "tail wag the dog" and count on a senseless performance appraisal system to provide career corrections for issues where the new employee failed to "get it right" during his or her training.

Point 7: Institute leadership.

Management is a natural for many people in the absence of the Deadly Diseases, which create unusual, suboptimizing responses from the employees. Performance appraisal and management by-the-numbers are the two worst culprits. This is not to say that there are not needs for basic supervisory training, but only after the Deadly Diseases have been mostly cured. Expecting seminars to enable your foremen to solve your problems for you in the presence of Deadly Diseases will provide many disappointments for you. After curing some of the Deadly Diseases, try a "Book of the Quarter Club." Upper management identifies very good books on management and organizational theory. Then copies are distributed among all the managers for their evaluation. At the risk of too many "quick fix" gimmicks, the managers are forced to remain in the philosophical, reflective mode about people. Each item in the reference list would be a good starting point, of course, after this book.

Point 8: Drive out fear.

There is no creativity or solving of system problems in the presence of fear. There is, however, ulcers and high blood pressure and corresponding deaths because of the instigator. Dismantling the by-the-numbers performance appraisal system, especially along with disallowing numerical quotas, will eliminate a large part of the fear in your organization. A few managers will leave because they love being the drill sergeant. Let them go! Help them find work with a competitor.

Point 9: Break down barriers between departments.

This is what teamwork is all about. It cannot exist, however, in an every-man-for-himself culture. Discontinue the numbers game. Start emphasizing the process that will help you continually improve. Hence, interdepartmental teams, statistical training, cross training in general, knowledge of the extended process, and some other stuff you already know about.

Point 13: Institute a vigorous program of education and self-improvement.

This is the training or retraining of the existing work force. The nurturing by a master can get to about 85 percent of your people. It starts with the statistical vision and then proceeds to broadening and extended process training. There must be follow-up by the master. The numbers game cannot be extinguished by just attending seminars.

There are some obstacles for which you must be prepared.

Obstacle 1: Search for examples.

No other firm is exactly like yours. The players are different. Upper management must be somewhat authoritative initially to get started dismantling the performance appraisal system. Unknowing managers may see the old system as a way to get "this employee thing" off their desks. They cannot deal with people. They need company-specific follow-up and nurturing.

Obstacle 2: Obsolescence in schools.

We do not teach teamwork in schools. We teach self-reliance and individual achievement. We even teach our children to be heroes, or else to be lost in the crowd. This subject may come later in a future book. For now, the problem is simply stated to let you see what you are "up against."

Obstacle 3: Poor teaching of statistical methods in industry.

The statistical training must be performed by a master who also knows something about your business. The insiders will never accept a novice when dealing with an issue as sensitive as performance appraisals or pay.

Obstacle 4: "Our troubles lie in the work force."

Between 85 and 98 percent of the problems in any firm are within the system. The local employees are powerless to make lasting improvements. This seems unbelievable to some people, and did to the author 10 years ago. Not now — I have seen too much to disbelieve! Why do the employees at times seem thoughtless and apathetic? Because of many embedded system problems. The two largest contributors are numerical quotas and numerically based performance appraisal systems. Be prepared to discuss some explicit examples with your colleagues. It is simple to find them. Do this now.

Obstacle 5: False starts.

Do not dismantle an old, dehumanizing, numerically based performance appraisal system in several steps. Cure this Deadly Disease all at once, and now. A halfway attempt will have little noticeable effect and will discredit your efforts.

When your firm is ready to begin the transition to world class and to eventually raise your profitability to 150 to 200 percent of its present level, you will have to start with visionary training. Then in one fell swoop, dismantle the numerically based performance system as discussed in this chapter. Then eliminate management by-the-numbers as discussed in Chapter 4. Interdepartmental teams or something very similar must fill the void. The required implementation time varies. There will be some noticeable improvement in about one year, considerable improvement in three years, and a total transition in about five to 10 years.

In some firms the negative effects of numerically based performance appraisals are defused because the sensitive managers just simply do not do what they are told to do by the corporate technocrats. They rank everyone the same and put in benign remarks for the solid citizens. This expensive, useless administrative waste will continue until upper management guarantees continued employment to the corporate paper handlers of these appraisals, and then cures the Deadly Disease. It has been said that this new approach seems like communism, where no individualized effort can be exceptionally rewarded. This is nonsense. Of course, solid citizens differ, and eventually the above average ones will exceed and be rewarded; but this is in the long term. There are too many system issues clouding the process in the short term, and solid citizens do not differ enough to be singled out in the short term to be ranked or categorized. Removal of the mistake-prone, demoralizing, numerically based performance appraisal will enhance teamwork and keep morale higher, both of which will enable the "cream to rise to the top" quicker before exiting the firm or becoming demoralized.

A friend once asked, what should I put in place of the numerical performance appraisal system and MBO? Deming's response: "Why replace one Disease with another?" Let creativity flourish through your newly founded teams. Does it surprise you that none of the 80 Nobel Prize recipients from the United States were under the scrutiny of a formal performance appraisal system? Is there ever a time and place for numerical performance appraisal systems and management by-the-numbers? Of course there is. When things are terrible, you know not what to do, and when the long term is of no consequence! If you sense a real desire to be judgmental on a periodic basis, look to the root-cause problem. Employees need frequent coaching and feedback. Start developing your style to provide it in a real-time fashion.

Numerically based performance appraisal is the most cherished of the "sacred cows." Only upper management can destroy this horrible practice. If you are powerless to do anything here, send an anonymous copy of this book to the people who are in charge. Direct them to this chapter. There's a lot of talk these days about process management of the organizational interfaces among the functional departments, and much of it is good. Elimination of the suboptimizing practice of numerical departmental quotas and the demoralizing by-the-numbers performance appraisal system will enhance teamwork and should be a precursor to any other effort to improve organizational performance. In fact, if these two Deadly Diseases are present, most other actions will, at best, be only minimally effective.

Now it is time to hear about another Deadly Disease.

6

LACK OF CONSTANCY
OF PURPOSE
DEADLY DISEASE 3

There seems to be considerable confusion over the lack of constancy of purpose Deadly Disease. Perhaps it's the name that Dr. Deming chose; or maybe it is the lack of upper management insight possessed by most upwardly mobile career hopefuls. In any event, the purpose of this chapter is to enable you to understand what constancy of purpose is, and what needs to be accomplished in the typical organization.

In philosophical terms, constancy of purpose exists when the culture, and mood, are such that the day-to-day, routine decisions of all managers and employees enhance the long-term survival of the firm, with no exceptions. Long-term survival means two things:

1. Lifetime employment of the team members.
2. Fanatical attention to quality and service to ensure lifetime markets.

Can firms guarantee lifetime employment? Of course not! In fact a legal guarantee is extremely rare even in Japan, despite what you hear. The point is that if day-to-day decisions are based on the real desire to permanently employ the entire work force and to keep all customers forever, all other indicators of performance will fall into line. In the long term this is true for sure, and is true even in the short term, when all players are working mostly as a team. What constancy of purpose accomplishes is the discontinuance of conflicts facing many employees, almost on a daily basis. As an example, constancy of purpose exists when a production operator at 3 A.M. discovers that a test specimen is barely out-of-spec, but could be shipped and probably not noticed by the customer, yet he or she still does not release it. And there are no expected repercussions by management. To ship this marginal product would jeopardize the long-term survival of the firm. We may not meet the day's quota, but tomorrow we do not have to worry about losing this customer's business with the resulting loss of jobs. Another example of constancy of purpose: The salesclerk at the hardware store willingly, no questions asked, returns your money because you are not satisfied. Perhaps a few dollars are lost today; however, the customer's repeat business and spreading of the good word brings in many more future profits than were seemingly lost today. There's no worry of repercussions by management. Another typical example was provided by one of the author's paper mill buddies. The portion of the machine upon which the pulp fibers are deposited, to be eventually pressed and dried into paper, is called the fabric. These expensive fabrics have a finite life, after which the finished product paper is eventually defective. A new fabric generally yields a very good finished product. There is, however, a period just before the "death" of a fabric when paper can be produced, but at a reduced internal production rate and deteriorated level of quality. Many of these resulting marginal quality characteristics do not have quantifiable or qualitative customer specs. However, the paper produced on the elderly fabric "is just not right," to quote a disenchanted customer. The customers can generally use the product, but only with noticeable operational inefficiency and fitness for use discrepancies. In the typical paper mill they run these fabrics right up to the "ragged-edge" because of the expense of the part and the loss of tonnage during the downtime resulting from the installation of a new fabric. Why? It is to meet the daily (weekly) production quotas, to elicit an "attaboy" from the mill manager, and to stay within budget. Detailed, scientific studies would show that the loss of production and marginal quality in the hands of the customer during the final, deteriorated hours of fabric use far outweigh the myopically gained short-term gains. Constancy of purpose in this case would involve management's scientific determination of the exact quality life of a typical fabric and making it company policy *(no exceptions)* that after this exact period of time, the old fabric be replaced with a new one. Enforced daily quotas, however, will not allow this. The hourly production operators want to retire worn fabrics because of pride of workmanship. (Let me tell you in no uncertain terms, 97 percent of American workers are absolutely wonderful! I talk to them practically every day.) Management often will not let them do what they know is right. The workers are told in this case to run the fabrics as long as possible to maximize tonnage, and that they had better meet the budgeted quota with no bad quality. It is impossible to do all this! There is no constancy of purpose. The operators and foremen are subjected to constant job stress. Sometimes they die prematurely from job-related stress! In some cases, more enlightened managers tell me that, "I have never told them to do that!" However, the pressure culture is there. It takes overt, opposite direction pressure to change things.

Some comments follow pertaining to how management can enhance the constancy of purpose. But first a few comments on order of implementation. Most of the management gurus say that all this cultural and constancy of purpose stuff by upper management must precede all other efforts pertaining to the Deadly Diseases and the 14 Points. The author totally disagrees. All the upcoming suggestions for upper management in this chapter will appear to the employees as senseless jawboning if there is still a strong by-the-numbers emphasis and a quantitative performance appraisal system. Also, the organizational members need to see overt management actions before they hear too many words. Obviously, the needed cultural changes must be set into motion before too long. A typical effective time line may proceed something like this:

1. Immediately: Visionary training is provided by a street-wise master pertaining to the Deming philosophy. All players must know what is coming. Upper management sits at the head table during the entire two-day session. The boss is prepared to discuss examples. He or she does not sit there nervously for 30 minutes, and then rush out to catch a plane.
2. Within a few months: The quantitative performance appraisal system is abruptly dismantled and replaced as discussed in Chapter 5. Formal MBO programs are discontinued.
3. After the next performance appraisal cycle: They believe something is going to happen now. Destroy the last remnants of MBO and management by-the-numbers.
4. Within half a year: Make the changes recommended in the remaining parts of this chapter pertaining to constancy of purpose.

Curing all five Deadly Diseases and implementation of all 14 Points overlap considerably, and the benefits in one area help in others. However, to change 40-year-old habits, one must proceed in a carefully planned and timed manner. Items 1 through 4 above seem to be phased properly for most firms. Now, for suggestions on what to do, pertaining to the lack of constancy of purpose Deadly Disease.

Most firms have mission statements. However, ask to see it and the typical lower-level manager has never heard of it; the middle managers saw it once and don't remember what was in it; the upper managers can probably dust off a copy for you. Why is there so little concern over this potentially powerful, but useless document? One reason is because of the useless garbage written within them. You know, things like:

- Maximize ROI.
- Reasonable return to stockholders.
- Maximum return to stockholders.
- Safety at all costs.
- Maximize P/E ratio.
- Zero defects.

- One hundred percent within specifications.
- Customer service.
- Customer satisfaction.

Obviously, all of these things are important, but a strong culture already exists to keep our attention directed to these issues. But more important, these types of considerations are not a mission. They are end results. To concentrate on them does not give organizational members guidance when facing conflicting demands in their daily activities. To concentrate on these types of things are like "the tail wagging the dog," or simply bottom-line management. This is useless, wishful thinking, even though admirable. If we have learned anything over the last 10 years pertaining to competing with the Japanese and other progressive international competitors, it is that we *must* emphasize the process, not the end result. We must put our efforts into identifying and improving the process needed to maximize ROI, as an example, not simply quoting ROI targets. If we do so correctly, we hardly have to even mention the numerical end results. Managing by-the-numbers generally elicits unwanted, or at least unpredictable, results. This was the message of this entire book up to this point.

The corporate mission statement must be process oriented and provide direction to the hourly operator or salesclerk who has to make a decision at 3 A.M. pertaining to whether or not to ship questionable product. A typical and recommended example for a mission statement:

> The mission of XYZ Company is to enhance employee job security through providing maximum quality and service to all customers. There will be no compromises on quality or service at any time, at anyone's request. No exceptions will be tolerated. Continual improvement of process and product are a requirement.

Notice the simplicity and the guidance given to all employees. If this philosophy seems unrealistic now, you are not alone in your thoughts (even though you are wrong!). In the absence of the Deadly Diseases and with true team players working through interdepartmental teams to get to most of the real issues that lead to the compromising situations, this mission is rather simple to achieve. Think about the stress the mission statement relieves. Note that "no exceptions will be tolerated." Removal of all this stress and the harnessing of the heretofore wasted related energy will, in some cases, prevent most problems from continuing to surface in the future.

Management must be emphatic in popularizing and enforcing this mission. It will be a rocky road at first. There will be many opportunities for you to make believers by example. Remember, "no exceptions will be tolerated." An executive told me once that they could not afford to rework an entire shipment of questionable product before shipping it. But they could, and they did! The follow-up shipment was late, but the customer was impressed at their honesty. Realizing the intensity of the new corporate mission, the team players quickly organized an interdepartmental team to establish procedures to prevent future occurrences of this type of problem, versus waiting for the emergency. They were able to take the time and energy to do this since they did not have to justify their self-worth on a daily basis to meet the budgeted quota. Net result: a 50 percent reduction in customer complaints, a 20 percent reduction in product variability, a 10 percent increase in average daily production. By golly, Phil Crosby was correct when he said "quality is free"; and I was right when I told a client that they can "have their cake and eat it too!" Their old bottom-line approach was previously making life impossible. Employees everywhere tell the author that they are demoralized because of being forced to do things they know are not right, such as shipping marginal product, or passing on problems to the next work crew so that they can meet the supervisor's daily quota.

The best companies in America have strong missions, often called superordinate goals, such as the following:

General Electric: *Progress is our most important product.*

Continental Bank: *We will find a way.*

Augusta College: *Georgia's premiere teaching institution.*

The top executives should spend about half their time communicating this mission and monitoring adherence to it. To quote Brian Joiner,

"Things do not move up organizations very well."[28] The only decision for an upper manager is: Does it fit our culture? With a unified corporate effort and previously unheard of teamwork, they have time to attend to this issue. Eventually, most of their heretofore day-to-day disruptive and administrative time wasters do not exist.[29] People finally know what their jobs are!

It is desirable to obtain considerable input prior to establishing the mission statement. It is, however, the responsibility and prerogative for upper management to design the document. To quote a statement made during a seminar by Ken Blanchard of *One-Minute Manager* fame, "The organization chart must be turned upside-down for most of your implementation; however, it remains right-side-up when establishing the corporate mission."

The author has never seen a case where some of the Deadly Diseases are not present. The employees express that there are many actions that they must take to enhance constancy of purpose that at times draw negative criticism from management. Examples include scrapping a marginal lot, but failing to meet the daily shipment quota, going over budget for preventive maintenance when the process had to be refurbished to enable it to make acceptable product, etc. Employees should not have to live with this stress.

Please take note again that a suitable corporate mission statement cannot be quantitative. As evidence, consider the study of 80 firms with strong (not necessarily good) mission statements. Eighteen were qualitative like the good ones of page 143; the rest were quantitative missions like "to maximize P/E ratio or 18 percent ROI." All 18 firms with enforced and good qualitative mission statements were outstanding performers compared with industry norms. None of the firms with strong quantitative missions were statistically significantly above industry norms. Bottom-line management simply does not work, even though at times it seems that it would.

The effective mission statement eliminates some of the conflicts and resulting stress in the organization. It provides unquestionable guidance when compromising situations arise. Management makes the mission statement effective by designing a good one and then emphatically enforcing it, but only after the "numbers game" has been discontinued. A month after it is revealed to all managers through every medium possible, especially through one-on-one contact, the CEO should be able to walk into any installation, address any first-line manager, and find that this person knows the mission statement and has already used it for guidance. This practice of following through is highly recommended. Also, recruits should be screened based on the mission statement. Customers should be aware of the new commitment. Be on the lookout for customers who can provide evidence of the mission statement not working. After half a year, if you have been totally effective, in response to the question, "Why are we in business?" most of your managers should say something like, "For customer satisfaction," or "To stay in business for life." The wrong answer is "to make a profit." This is a by-the-numbers, bottom-line approach.

Without a unifying mission and superordinate qualitative goals, too many private agendas will exist and underhanded internal competition may exist. Certainly, there will be numerous knee-jerk reactions that increase variability and rob the solid citizens of their pride of workmanship. Effective elevating corporate goals are the "glue" that binds it all together. Very few firms have this.

The mission statement and its staunch support are important parts of constancy of purpose. Now some additional ideas follow that are related to constancy of purpose, but somewhat different. Remember, constancy of purpose consists of those things that we do to enhance our continued profitable existence far into the future. We have to take orchestrated, overt action to make this happen for the long term. Do not worry too much about the equally important short term. It will take care of itself! It always has; it always will! If you are a top executive and do not spend a considerable part of your time looking 10 years ahead, either you are remiss, or else your firm and its hundreds of private agendas are preventing you from doing the real work of top executives. In either case, the Deming philosophy transition must begin.

The next issue pertaining to constancy involves creating a family spirit among all employees. In the normal case, families stick together. (Of course this does not cover libidinous 13-year-olds whose hormones and general hate of everything make them act like aliens for about two years!) With a well-orchestrated mission and effective interdepartmental teams, firms should (and can) view themselves more as families. Here are a few suggestions:

1. Cross-functional training for new hires. This includes basic training and upper management testimonials on the corporate mission as well as considerable stints in sales, manufacturing, line, and staff. No shortcuts here; no heavy reliance on uncoordinated OJT. Show these people up front how important they are. You likely need to redo this phase for your present work force. You want the synergy of a true team. We should understand other departments' problems. Initially expensive? Yes, but the ROI will be about 1,000 percent for this training.

2. Never cut any group's pay and not others. According to Gitlow and Gitlow, in 1983, Greyhound cut labor's pay by an average of 7.8 percent while management got raises averaging approximately the same amount. They needed the Deming vision prior to that time; however, history is cruel. Practically no one had the vision prior to that time, certainly not the author. At the time of this writing, Greyhound is "paying the piper." They have many private agendas. The firm is presently in shambles. In contrast, in Japan, the sacrificial pecking order for hard times is: reduction in dividends first; followed by decreases in upper management pay, then middle management, then lower management, then labor, then the training budget, then layoffs. There are no exceptions! (Notice that the training budget is near the bottom of this hit list.)

3. Employee stock ownership plans must be considered. According to Levering, a 1986 study of 45 companies by the National Center for Employee Ownership showed that firms with employee stock ownership plans grew 7.1 percent faster than their industry norms. A comment made in jest and overheard by the author: "My biggest error was buying

stock in the company! Now I worry about the lousy product I make and ship!''

4. Promote health and fitness through fitness centers.

5. Authorize flexible hours. The author remembers the personal turmoil when it came time to renew his driver's license or to babysit while his wife went to the dentist. Useless stress! I quit that job!

6. Training should be ongoing, versus always in response to a problem. This sends the message to the work force that they are important and a permanent asset, not a short-term liability.

Industry executives say that the new young workers they are hiring are wimpy. This may be true. But in any event, we old war-veteran, recession-or-depression-beaten, school-of-hard-knocks, tough guys are a dying breed. The corporation must be reinvented to inspire for the future. According to John Welch, Jr., CEO of General Electric[30]: ''The pace of the 90s will make the 80s look like a picnic — a walk in the park. Competition will be relentless. The bar of excellence in everything we do will be raised every day.''

There must be a heretofore unthought of drive to enhance constancy of purpose. All players should have the same agenda. A few more general action item examples:

1. Start a major drive to reduce variability. This involves variability in product characteristics, service, treatment of employees, costs, etc. At the risk of becoming an unmanageable bureaucracy (which is impossible when there is cost competition), reducing variability always reduces problems. Try asking operating managers to report variability measures to upper managers, versus the normal bottom-line figures. See Fellers for some theoretical background.

2. Celebrate the small improvements to quality, service, or costs. The hero-hopefuls are all looking for ''home runs.'' We have to learn to reward players and teams for ''singles and doubles.'' A major contrast of the American and Japanese business cultures is the Japanese ability to

continually improve a bit at a time. We all want to be John Wayne and "take the hill in one fell swoop in a heroic fashion." But this seldom works these days. Talk to your people about the new mode. Learn to reward group performance. Do nothing to foster internal competition that makes it look as if some can win at the expense of others. Sure, you may seemingly lose a "drop" here and there. However, through teamwork you will begin to reap "buckets full" of success later.

3. Never forego preventive maintenance or upkeep of any office or plant equipment. The "knowns" quantified by the financial wizards are far outweighed by the "unknowns." You cannot quantify the impact that it has on the solid citizens when they (finally) see management maintaining the equipment well and letting pride of workmanship manifest itself. There should be no budget limitations on preventive maintenance. There should be no ROI analysis for opportunities to improve quality, to enhance customer satisfaction, or to increase pride of workmanship. Just do it! The unknown and unknowable paybacks are five to 10 times the value of the measurables. How do I know? I was there, and I have been patient enough a few times to wait for and to count these long-term returns.

4. Continually update your perception of what the customer thinks. Never forego an opportunity to improve quality or service. Forget about the cost-benefit calculations! Do not rely solely on customer complaints. This is useful information, but from a nonrandom sample of people. Use a marketing research expert to help you get in touch with the "typical" customer.[31]

5. Do not be afraid to develop and market test "blue sky" ideas. Research on existing customers is never complete. Whoever asked for microwave ovens, telephones, or hula hoops? Someone said, "Look what we developed. How do you like it?"

6. Do not let the managers lose touch with the basic business. Consider a system similar to Walt Disney World's "cross utilization process" where all managers spend one week per year in theme costumes doing menial work. You will not believe what your executives learn.

Upper management has "gotten a bad rap" pertaining to this constancy of purpose issue. They really do try to give top priority to long-term survival. Several studies have revealed this fact, along with hundreds of personal observations. Why does it look otherwise to the corporate insiders looking up at them? First, the upper managers often do not know what to do. Perhaps this book will give them some insight. Second, not knowing what to do and thus leaving the by-the-numbers approach intact makes upper management seem to be interested in nothing but the bottom line, whether this is the case or not. Third, they feel that if they let their natural, nurturing, coaching tendencies surface, they will be viewed by their superiors as weak and ineffective. A carefully orchestrated transition by the Deming vision will help prevent this misconception.

The following list of Deming's 14 Points apply here to enhance constancy of purpose:

Point 1: Create constancy of purpose toward improvement of product and service, with the aim to become competitive and to stay in business, and to provide jobs.

Enough said! Point 1 and Deadly Disease 3 are the same subject.

Point 2: Adopt the new philosophy. We are in a new economic age. Western management must awaken to the challenge, must learn its responsibilities, and take on leadership for a change.

This point confuses us at times. At a minimum it means that you must implement the preceding chapters of this book. It also means that there will never be any further acceptance of poor quality or service reaching the customer. This "nature of the beast" verbiage and acceptance of failures are never to be tolerated again. Of course, defects will still occur, but defective products are never shipped; and in all cases, the road map to correction is constructed and traveled. It takes time to get to the root causes. Quotas do not allow time.

Point 5: Improve, constantly and forever, the system of production and service, to improve quality and productivity, and thus constantly decrease costs.

The phrase "continual improvement" must become common language around the firm. Remember the "singles versus home run" analogy. We must accept and celebrate the small stream of continual improvements that can come from better teamwork. Everyone is presently trying to be a high roller going for the big haul, the home run. There simply are not many home runs left. There never were many! We must have the continual stream of improvements. Some firms are using as yearly objectives, "Just show me you are improving." If everyone is continually improving the system, you are there! The same applies to cost. Over hundreds of projects, I have yet to see one where a proper approach to quality improvement did not also reduce costs. When there are short-term numerical objectives, it is difficult for a person's boss to get excited about subtle process improvements that will take many months to add up to a noticeable impact. After several turn-offs by the boss, the workers resign themselves to just following instructions. They give up! The firm loses millions of dollars worth of future improvements. You would not believe what the workers in the trenches tell the author!

Point 8: Drive out fear, so that everyone may work effectively for the company.

The mission statement in practice can help do this by limiting the number of conflicting options. There may be other things that can be accomplished such as coaching managers against making threats. Take some advice from me and my mentors who have made a living conducting seminars and training sessions for many years. As soon as you threaten folks with statements like, "If we don't do better, the Japanese will take over our market," their eyes become glassy and you have lost them. Keep everything positive. There is no creativity and enhanced teamwork with fear. People love a challenge.

Point 9: Break down barriers between departments. All the stuff in the previous chapters helps do this.

Point 14: Put everybody in the company to work to accomplish the transformation. It is everybody's job.

This book is not only for manufacturing. Include all functions in your mission statement, communications, and visionary training. The main reasons that you do not hear about more non-manufacturing successes pertaining to the Deming vision are two-fold:

1. Everybody started in manufacturing.
2. The gurus and coaches must get much closer to the detailed processes in administration to make a positive impact. The same principles apply; however, the output/input payback may be a bit lower, so firms have taken a wait-and-see attitude about non-manufacturing analyses for quality and service improvements. It is time to quit "waiting" and to begin to "see."

Several obstacles should be considered and planned before attacking the lack of constancy of purpose Deadly Disease.

Obstacle 1: Hope for instant pudding.

Cultures change very slowly. The players with a long-term commitment must be dedicated to make it happen. Do not expect too much from an employee with one year left until retirement.

Obstacle 2: Our problems lie entirely in the work force.

Never! Never! Never! It is the numbers game, no action plan for long-term survival, and no road map for solving system problems.

Obstacle 3: False starts.

As stated at the beginning of this chapter, stabilize the internal competition and knee-jerk responses somewhat before going to work on the culture and constancy of purpose. Do this by dismantling the numbers orientation.

Obstacle 4: The supposition that it is only necessary to meet specifications.

The only model for the future is continual improvement and variability reduction. The competition in the future is going to be "punishing." Some of your competitors are going to take the lead and improve 10 to 20 percent every year. Miss no opportunities to improve quality, service, productivity, and costs. Forget the cost-benefit financial analyses. Work only from the recommendation of interdepartmental teams to minimize your errors. These teams will generally try not to "throw money" at your problems. Solutions are often free through improved methods, closer relations with vendors, SPC, cross training, brainstorming, etc.

As the famed football coach George Allen once stated, "No one can beat 11 men pulling in the same direction in a carefully orchestrated effort!" This is what constancy of purpose and the mission statement are all about.

7

MOBILITY OF MANAGEMENT DEADLY DISEASE 4

The tip of the iceberg pertaining to this mobility of management Deadly Disease is the constant movement of managers from one firm to another. The "ice below the water" that institutions need to address are the reasons behind this movement. Until fairly recently, many executives considered this situation to be somewhat benign and, even at times, desirable because of our mistaken perception of the professional manager. You know the guy who can "stop speeding bullets and leap tall buildings in a single bound." There are a few personal traits and universal tools that are easily transferable among firms; however, the last two decades of comparatively declining American productivity have taught us that the idea of the universal professional manager is certainly a myth. Administration skills and personal traits are fine, but add up to little as compared to process and industry knowledge. The days of systems and bottom-line, by-the-numbers management are gone. Effective managers today are into the "process" of continually improving. They know the "nuts and bolts." Managerial life is nowhere near as easy as it was perceived to be in the misleading 1950s and 1960s. People are considerably more complex than any bureaucratic, business school model ever considered. They are also much more fragile. The unknowns and unknowables that lead to superior long-term competitiveness cannot be measured numerically.

A carefully orchestrated transformation according to Dr. Deming's message will eventually eliminate the old, arcane adage that employee turnover, to a certain extent, is good because it brings in new blood. It actually is possible to keep your "old blood from growing anemic." Why do experienced newcomers (new blood) at times seem to be so insightful? For several reasons, the first of which is that they do not know enough about the political climate to have their good ideas thwarted. They just speak up! Second, they have seen different approaches work elsewhere. Third, they still have vivid memories of being dumped upon by their last employer. This makes them more empathetic in their new job, until our Diseases alienate them. The point here is that interdepartmental teams operating in the absence of the Deadly Diseases can accomplish all the innovative feats of an insightful newcomer. We really do not need new blood if we manage properly. Employee turnover should be considered bad in all cases once the Deming transformation is mostly complete. Low-side outliers do not fit; however, they should be identified and helped without our having to wait months or years for them to resign. We must face up to this issue!

Curing the Deadly Diseases will eliminate 75 percent of a firm's employee turnover. There are a few additional ideas worth consideration that can enhance your efforts to maintain an experienced work force. Several are listed below (I am sure you can add to this list):

1. Develop a long-term succession plan to enable an eventual policy of promotion only from within. A friend of the author works for a large firm that won a national award for so-called quality excellence. She explained to him that seemingly the only avenue into top management (with an unnoticeably few exceptions) was to put in about 10 productive years in the trenches. Then you must leave and get a broader exposure with another similar firm for five to 10 years. Then you return to this firm with a large

promotion. The loyal middle managers who never left are completely demoralized and have created an expensive, protective bureaucracy to guard them against upper management and disgruntled lower managers.

2. Encourage career broadening, monotony reducing job rotation. Most firms are seemingly doing this; however, the author still hears hundreds of testimonials per year from bored employees who want to contribute more. They are boxed in by the bureaucratic organization chart. Interdepartmental teams will help here also.

3. Pay and vacation benefits should be highly correlated with years of service.

4. There should be continual industry salary surveys. The insiders must be brought into the industry ranges, and pay should be determined according to a pro rata formula based on seniority. Expect constant upheaval and mistake-prone newcomers if you must pay newcomers more money than the comparably skilled existing work force. There will be constant turnover. The problem existed prior to the arrival of the new employee as the firm drifted away from salary market values.

5. For all salaried employees, budget for required attendance at training seminars. About five days per year at seminars of their choice are recommended. If the boss makes you attend a workshop, it does not count as part of the five days.

6. There must be parallel career paths for technical professionals. It is despicable for top engineers to reach a pay plateau considerably below that of administrative managers who make similar contributions. American firms need experienced technical professionals who do not have to give up their trade to move into administration. This is a major and mostly American problem. Many system problems can (and should) be solved with inexpensive methods improvements, operating strategy changes, simple SPC, better teamwork, etc. It takes

experienced technical people to contribute to the identification of these "free" improvements. Young engineers (less than five years) and new MBAs are scared to embark on people-solutions to problems. What do they do? They seek out gadgets, computers, and numbers systems to provide the instant pudding. (Note two obstacles are referenced in this sentence!)

7. Consider flex-time and floating holidays. The 8-to-5, 50 weeks per year regimentation is punishing, and at times unnecessary.

8. Most organizations have one or two real psychopathic people punishers on the payroll. For some reason, a few people thrive on giving out orders and being domineering and punishing. Many of these bullies will flee during the Deming transformation. Help them find a way out! For the ones that stay, they must be removed from direct supervisory positions, and immediately. In this case, "one or two bad apples can destroy the entire barrel." Consider creating staff or advisory positions for them, or perhaps face-saving early retirements. Upper management tends to fail to own up to this distasteful task. The resulting cost is unbelievable!

9. Learn from former employees. On exit interviews people seldom "burn their bridges." They know that the truly bad guys of the world will come after them because they like taking advantage of people. Usually after one to three years when the former employee feels secure in his or her new job, he or she will talk. Set up a system to enable you to follow up one to three years later. You will not believe what you learn!

10. Be on the lookout for high turnover situations. Use the Pareto principle of Chapter 2. The author was once the third ex-military officer, college boy to exit a job in three years. Why? There was a technically capable retired master sergeant in the department who had paid his dues in the firm; however, just as the Air Force had done to him

for 22 demeaning years, the company kept sending in these "commissioned," inexperienced college boys to be the boss and to be trained by the sergeant. The sergeant made their OJT into a "smoke screen" and tactfully withheld enough information to make these new guys prone to mistakes. The sergeant was a master of deception. The author told all when he quit. The sergeant is still there doing sergeant stuff; they never promoted him. The eventual, permanent department manager was carefully selected not to "fit the mold" of the type of person the sergeant resented. The sergeant and the new manager were effectively coached at the outset. Be alert, this type of problem is typical.

11. There should be a careful job analysis of all open positions in the firm. Learn to screen applicants who do not fit or who may not like the job. Of course, all firms are trying to do this. However, few are doing it well. The corporate mission statement can help here. As an example, a lone wolf should know that he or she may not fit in the teamwork environment.

12. A recruit should understand clearly what the typical career paths are and how long one usually has to wait for promotions. The author hears about a hundred "if only I had knowns" per year.

13. Assume that all new hires are superstitiously trained. Visionary Deming training must be provided immediately. Have a visionary insider counsel them on their understanding and acceptance. Try to have a visionary insider screen the recruits to weed out the ones who will not be able to make the transition. Make them read this book prior to the job interview, then gauge their acceptance. New hires perceive an intense pressure to show quick improvements. Consequently, they are among the worst offenders when it comes to quick-fixes. Counsel them carefully and coach them on your culture.

14. Do a Pareto chart on employee turnover by supervisor. twenty percent of your supervisors probably cause 80 percent of your turnover. Elimination of the judgmental and/or numerically based performance appraisal system may help considerably here.

Unlike previous chapters, there will be no listing here of the relevant Points and Obstacles. They all apply here. There will be less mobility out of the firm when it is run properly in a humanistic fashion.

8

SHORT-TERM ORIENTATION DEADLY DISEASE 5

In many ways all the Deadly Diseases pertain to the typical manager being overly short-term oriented. However, most all the other Deadly Diseases can be cured with enough bad habits remaining to still leave an obsession with the short term, at the expense of the long term. The intent of this chapter is to tie up some of these "loose ends." Get one thing perfectly clear: The short term is extremely important, and there will be no long term without a careful strategy for the short term. Identification of this Deadly Disease by Dr. Deming was a managerial theory breakthrough, however, because it has enhanced the understanding of many converted practitioners of a heretofore little known fact: A well-orchestrated transformation of curing the Deadly Diseases, implementing the 14 Points, and heeding the Obstacles generally extinguishes the long-term/short-term trade-off. The results of the interdepartmental teams have achieved payback periods that satisfied even the most superstitiously trained bean-counters. Typical ROIs will be 300 to 1,000 percent; and these results are for only what you can count. The true returns, counting the unknowns and unknowables, will be five to 10 times greater. Pertaining to issues of quality, service, and employee pride of workmanship, the gains (losses) you think you have experienced are only about one-tenth to one-fifth of the total.[32] The use of ROI, internal rate of return, or NPV formulas are very misleading when applied to issues that impact quality, employee pride of workmanship, and customer satisfaction. A calculated ROI of 15 percent for projects affecting these issues is probably only the tip of the iceberg. The real short-term return is probably closer to 30 percent, with a total long-term return of about 75 percent.

The financial wizards at times are strangling the life out of the line employees who are trying to manufacture a product or provide a service. Consider the quote pertaining to Robert McNamara, the leader of the financial Whiz Kids, who originally helped but eventually almost ruined Ford Motor Company in the 1950s and 1960s[33]:

> Finance was soon a power of its own. Its principal driving force was Robert McNamara, and its basic philosophy was: whatever the product men and manufacturing men want, deny it. Make them sweat and then make them present it again, and once again delay as long as possible. If in the end it has to be granted, cut it in half. Always make them fight the balance sheet, and always put the burden on them. That way, they will always be on the defensive and will think twice about asking for anything.

This reference pertained to Ford during the 1950s; it is no longer that way, I am sure. However, during the period of 1950 to 1970, when the Whiz Kids had their way to prop up the short term at the expense of the long term, the Japanese automakers were continually improving product and process. There was no calculated effort in Japan to cure the Deadly Diseases; they never had developed them in the first place. Prominent names like Deming, Juran, and Ishikawa were there to teach them the statistical approach.

Now back to the quote. It is still similar to this quote in the typical firm. Many engineers and operational managers tell me that they spend approximately 10 percent of their time trying to justify the approval of "must do" projects that will have a profound impact on the survivability of the firm. One of the author's visionary process engineering buddies said of the financial types, "You ride herd, you resubmit, you persist, you wear them down, and eventually they cave in." Think of all the wasted energy! Obviously, financial prudence is a good thing; however, there is a limit. You cannot quantify the unknown and unknowables. As an example, who can quantify the behavioral impact of management finally repairing something that has been malfunctioning and causing the employees headaches for years, and/or causing questionable product quality? You may say that you have no situations like this in your firm. You do! This type of information you get is filtered. In working with interdepartmental teams, the author has seen situations that you would not believe! Pumps malfunctioning, temperature probes that do not work, product guides that have to be held in place by an operator with her foot, outdated forms that newcomers cannot understand, pipes leaking, and demoralizing the work force! Why? You cannot calculate the bureaucratically required ROI on these issues; the supervisor will miss a week's numerical quota if he disrupts the work flow to take action; if it does not shut down the process, the maintenance manager will let it get out-prioritized, etc. The employees and the customers get calculated out within our present financial system.

Please do not be misled by the emphatic examples. Financial return calculations are fine for many proposed investments, but not for moderate or minor investments that impact quality, customer service, or employee morale. The company regulations must be rewritten and strongly popularized by upper management. Request for approval of projects that fit into one of the three categories discussed above must not be subjected to the numbers game. You cannot quantify the unknowns and unknowables that are five to 10 times as profitable as the measurable income flows where quality, customer service, or pride of workmanship are involved. A strong rationale for using interdepartmental teams is to bypass the financial capital budgeting game. Put a finance person on the team. Make sure the team leader is knowledgeable of budgetary constraints. And make sure that upper management has agreed to follow all their recommendations.

Deming said to never disapprove any opportunity to improve

product or service, or to reduce variability. From what the author has seen, following this recommendation would produce eventual financial returns beyond what you could ever believe at this point. However, the bureaucratic and finance-oriented nature of most firms makes this commitment impossible, at least for five more years until the Deming transformation is mostly complete. An interim necessity is to exempt interdepartmental team recommendations from the bean-counter approval cycle and to create a new category of proposed expenditures that include recommendations below a certain dollar figure that involve apparent improvements in quality, customer service, or employee job satisfaction. This new category may be named something like quality enhancers, or variability reducers. Flaunt this new procedure! Do not assume that people get the word when a Deadly Disease is cured. Publicize the fact.

Another extremely important issue relating to this short-term Deadly Disease is that of vendor selection. The old business school recommendation of the 1960s was to purchase from as many vendors as possible. Keep them hungry. Keep the price down because of competition. Only give short-term contracts to keep them on their toes. Keep an arm's-length, adversarial relationship to retain your objectivity. In many firms, it takes reams of paperwork and disgusting amounts of time to get permission to buy from other than the low-cost bidder. To the uninformed, nonvisionary mind, all this garbage makes sense. But there are few (if any) exceptions to the fact that this is a despicable, extremely expensive attitude. Many firms can attest to this fact. (Can you believe that most elevators are bought from the low-cost bidder?) For example, a food products company bought cans from three acceptable vendors. The operators continually complained about the lost production time resulting from having to readjust the machines when a new box of cans from a different vendor was loaded onto the machines. The purchasing manager stated emphatically that, "They are all in spec!" And they were; but in ways, most of which were unquantifiable, the vendors were different. It took about six months to establish the best of the three acceptable vendors. All of the business was given to the best supplier. The yearly savings from reduced downtime alone was almost $1 million per year.[34]

Ford has reduced the number of vendors of 60 percent of its steel products from about six suppliers to one sole source. The typical Kimberly-Clark Kleenex® plant has reduced the number of corrugated container vendors from about six to one or two. IBM used to contract with 190 carriers to move parts around the country. This created thousands of invoices and few carriers who had enough IBM business for them to be totally committed to the long-term survival of the company, versus their own short-term struggle. IBM now has nine carriers (versus 190), and the recordable savings is $20 million per year. You want to hear more? The ultra-modern GM Saturn plant has only 170 vendors, versus the typical unwieldly 800 of other GM car assembly plants. Their JIT would not have been possible if it had not been for the long-term vendor partnerships with this smaller, more manageable number of vendors. Many transition-hopefuls have misunderstood Deming's recommendations here. "Sole sourcing" is the goal. In reality, what is usually practical is simply "fewer" vendors, chosen in a discerning manner. What usually happens is to have three versus 10, or 10 versus 25. With a smaller number, there may be time to nurture the vendor partners. The list of advantages goes on, and the same findings prevail. Twice as many vendors, twice as many problems. The author has been involved in numerous components of variance statistical studies in manufacturing. The findings of these studies revealed that the fraction of the finished product variability resulting from multiple vendors was from 30 to 95 percent. A typical figure was about 70 percent. From an engineering perspective, vendors vary among themselves. The among-vendor variability is generally five to 10 times the worst within-vendor deviations. Of course, the goal is to scientifically choose the best one or two vendors; however, it is not uncommon to find that sole sourcing with the worst vendor is better than back-and-forth switching among them all. Believe it or not!

From a business perspective (whatever that is!), reducing the number of vendors makes good sense. Some typical costs of multiple sourcing are:

- Excessive travel costs visiting multiple sources.
- Increased paperwork.
- High telephone bills.
- Loss of volume discounts.
- Larger risks of security leaks.
- Many machine setups.
- Big inventory safety stocks.

Furthermore, the sole vendor's overhead can be spread over a larger volume. In the typical case they are willing to give you volume discounts beyond those published in their catalogs. Price usually comes down with reducing the number of vendors. Quality always improves.

With only a few trusted vendors with long-term contracts, the concept of the extended process starts coming to life. The vendor's technical problems are also the customer's, and vice versa. In many ways, they work as the same company. They share information and help each other continually improve. The survival of each is dependent upon the other. Heretofore seemingly insurmountable problems are solved. There's very little protective behavior. This concept of sole sourcing is already happening in this country. The author has been in the middle of dozens of these so-called vendor-customer partnerships. The results are unbelievable. Barriers are finally removed. Consider, as an example, the scientific instruments industry. According to Deming, through vendor-customer partnerships, 75 percent of the recent innovations have come from user recommendations. These kinds of results would have never occurred under the old model of adversarial, arm's-length treatment of vendors where price was given the most (only) consideration. It is hard to even imagine the adverse impact of the adversarial, lowest-cost purchasing behavior of the past. Consider mass transit in America as reported by Deming. Because of erratic performance of equipment purchased on the basis of price alone, expansion of mass transit in this country has been retarded by a generation.

The price tag is too easy to read! But what can the purchasing employees do in the absence of a technical understanding of the needs of the process? Not very much! They must be trained and nurtured. The users of all purchased parts must have a say in who gets the contract. People must be appraised on reducing the number of vendors, and by how they do it. By all means never give people quantitative, MBO-type objectives pertaining to how many vendors must be culled by the end of the year. This would be a self-defeating endeavor. Who knows how many vendors we can identify as good and bad? It generally takes about 18 months to effectively evaluate and compare vendors. Then it takes about three years to nurture these customer-vendor partnerships to totally reap the full financial impact of this undertaking. As you can see, this transition does not fit any sort of year-to-year reporting system that we have grown accustomed to. Contrary to the common practices of having to get approval for not taking the lowest price, for not buying from multiple vendors, or for entering into a contract for more than one year, everything should be the opposite. One should have to get approval for doing otherwise. Will the purchasing people like this? Of course not, until they know that their paychecks are secure, and until they accept the Deming vision. It generally takes about five years to transform the purchasing function. Retirements of superstitiously trained purchasing old-timers helps, especially when they play golf and rub shoulders with too many of the vendors. It takes about 18 months to cull vendors who refuse to get into the Deming transition, SPC, etc. This culling must be done in a very fair, objective, data-based fashion. Or it may be as simple as asking the front-line employees. Many of the problem solving tools of Chapter 2 will be helpful here.

The typical American firm has started the transition toward sole sourcing, or at least reducing the number of vendors. If yours has not, this must begin immediately. It takes time.

A last issue for this short-term oriented Deadly Disease pertains to executive compensation. How can you expect an executive to make correct long-term oriented decisions when his bonus or compensation is connected very closely with this year's bottom line? You cannot, of course! Results-oriented pay is good; however, do not aggravate the long-term/short-term dilemma any more than it already is. Executive compensations and bonuses should be based on a three- to five-year moving average. This enables them to forego a few short-term gains for even more future profitability. The very top executives' retirement packages should be based mostly on corporate earnings three to five years after they leave. It is their job, while still working, to help create a culture that emphasizes constancy of purpose, or profits, well into the future. The following of the 14 Points are obviously applicable here.

Point 3: Cease dependence on inspection to achieve quality. Eliminate the need for inspection on a mass basis by building quality into the product in the first place.

The Point applies universally across the extended process, internal and external. It fits very well with the vendor issue of this chapter. You cannot inspect quality into a vendor's product as it enters your process. At the levels of competitive quality that are acceptable today, it is like "searching for the needle in the haystack" to do so. Any sort of frequential sampling plan like the military standards or the Dodge-Romig tables is nothing more than a bureaucratic crutch that is slightly better than nothing at all, but may be necessary until you and the vendor work as partners to prevent the occurrence of defects in the first place. This takes about 18 months to change in the normal case, and is not possible at all unless you are dealing with a small number of vendors.

Point 10: Eliminate slogans, exhortations, and targets for the work force asking for new levels of productivity and zero defects.

These banners and posters are directed toward the wrong people. Most of the problems are within the system and take a long-term orientation to solve. Posters are viewed as silly short sightedness by the front-line workers. Tear down all such banners immediately and prohibit their future use. Tell every employee that all goals for the future will be accompanied by a road map.

Following are several Obstacles to look out for:

Obstacle 1: Hope for instant pudding.

Believe it or not, very little of importance happens in the short term. There are many seemingly useful results in the short term; however, most are knee-jerk, suboptimizing gyrations that cannot last. The statistical vision, the Deming transition, and the interdepartmental teams produce long-term, world-class results.

Obstacle 2: Use of Military Standard 105D and other tables for acceptance.

A knowledgeable person in statistics can tell you that if you test a lot enough times, it has to pass eventually. Consider the manufacturing plant that used Military Standard 105D to release lots for shipment (any other acceptance sampling plan is almost as bad). When a lot failed the acceptance criteria, it was re-sampled by a higher authority. If it failed again, it was retested by an even higher authority. There were five levels of higher authority. Even with fair sampling and testing, which they were not doing, a statistician could tell you that a 75 percent defective lot would eventually pass one of the five boards, almost 100 percent of the time. What was the net result for this dinosaur company? In 15 years of operation, a lot had never been withheld from shipment, even though some were suspected to be 30 percent defective. It was recommended that they use SPC and related issues upstream in the process to get into the preventive mode. Final testing was destructive and they could not "search the haystack closely enough to find the needles." Also, why bother with the half-million dollar expense of after-the-fact testing? No lots had ever been withheld! Their response? Nothing! Now they have lost many of their markets.

One of the most progressive plant managers the author has known kept the employees tuned in to the long term by constantly asking questions of the sort, "Okay, enough about the leaking pump. Get it repaired. Now, let's talk about the projects that you are working on to enhance our survival five years down the road!" In the absence of the Deadly Diseases, this question was sure to make this facility a world-class Mecca within this large corporation over the years. It now is "five years later." Their costs, quality, and profits are unparalleled in their industry. It is hard for a newcomer to see why. Those of us who were there five years ago know why!

As this book is drawing to a close, it should be clear that this Deming transition is not for the meek, weak, or impatient. Deming has stated that the typical U.S. firm is operating at about 50 percent of its potential profitability. The author has seen enough to believe this. Bureaucracy, knee-jerk reactions, private agendas, suboptimization, and burnout is robbing us of our standard of living. Consider the brief parting remarks of the next chapter. Then begin the change process.

9

CLOSING REMARKS

I t is doubtful that anyone could grasp all of the material in this book at one sitting. It took the author almost 10 years of constant study, application, and reflection upon the issues to put this together as a comprehensive document. Let's call it Theory D in honor of Dr. Deming.[35] Actually, it is his theory. Reflect upon his material for a few days. Then go back and study every word again. Perhaps read a few of the references. Then immediately go to work. First, dismantle performance appraisal by-the-numbers, then abolish management mostly by-the-numbers (follow up well here), create a communicated effective corporate mission statement to enhance constancy of purpose, review corporate practices that aggravate management mobility, and encourage long-term thinking, especially toward vendor selection. In other words, implement Theory D. It will take time and patience.

Deming continues to learn and update his teachings every few years. The author humbly stumbles onto new insights from time to time. It is almost exactly 10 years since this country was exposed to Dr. Deming through mass media. In about five years from now after the Deming transition is more complete, and the present interest in total quality management (TQM), world-class manufacturing, continuous improvement, etc., materializes, a follow-up to this volume will be forthcoming. Please send me your examples so we can all learn together.

Deming was overheard once stating that the typical firm could conceivably double its bottom-line profit. This comment seems a bit outrageous until one considers the fact that at least 50 percent of the manpower input for most firms involves politicking, supporting private agendas, career managing, CYA-ing, needlessly documenting, boss watching, excessively having to "make the boss look good," etc. The Deming transition will eventually eliminate much of this activity. Then more employee effort "goes to the bottom line."

APPENDIX A
THE 14 POINTS

Ways managers should act to create the correct culture, sense of purpose, reduced fear, and reduced inhibitors to change:

1. Create constancy of purpose toward improvement of product and service, with the aim to become competitive and to stay in business.
2. Adopt the new philosophy. We are in a new economic age. Western management must awaken to the challenge, must learn its responsibilities, and take on leadership for change.
3. Drive out fear so that everyone may work effectively for the company.

Specific actions managers must take to promote team effort:

6. Institute training on the job. (Never use OJT as a sole training tool.)
7. Institute leadership. The aim of supervision should be to help people and machines and gadgets do a better job. Supervision of management is in need of an overhaul, as well as supervision of production workers.

10. Eliminate slogans, exhortations, and targets for the work force asking for zero defects and new levels of productivity. Such exhortations only create adversarial relationships, as the bulk of the causes of low quality and low productivity belong to the system and thus lie beyond the power of the work force.

11. (a) Eliminate work standards (quotas) on the factory floor. Substitute leadership.

    (b) Eliminate management by objectives. Eliminate management-by-the-numbers, numerical goals. Substitute leadership.

12. Remove barriers that rob the hourly worker of his or her right to pride of workmanship. The responsibility of supervisors must be changed from sheer numbers to quality.

13. Institute a vigorous program of training and retraining.

Decisions pertaining to job and organization design:

8. Cease dependence on inspection to achieve quality. Eliminate the need for inspection on a mass basis by building quality into the product in the first place. No after-the-fact acceptance sampling.

4. End the practice of awarding business on the basis of price tag. Instead minimize total cost. Move toward a single supplier for any one item, on a long-term relationship of loyalty and trust. This does not mean that there must always be sole sourcing. Three vendors instead of twelve may be the answer.

5. Improve constantly and forever the system of production and service, to improve quality and productivity, and thus constantly decrease costs.

9. Break down barriers between departments. People in research, design, sales, and production must work as a team to foresee production and use problems.

14. Create a top management structure to accomplish the transformation.

APPENDIX B
TYPICAL OBSTACLES

1. Hope for instant pudding.
2. The supposition that solving problems, automation, gadgets, and new machinery will transform industry.
3. Search for examples.
4. "Our problems are different."
5. Obsolescence in schools.
6. Poor teaching of statistical methods in industry.
7. Use of Military Standard 105D and other tables for acceptance.
8. "Our quality control department takes care of all our problems of quality."
9. "Our troubles lie entirely with the work force."
10. False starts.
11. "We installed quality control."
12. The unmanned computer.
13. The supposition that it is necessary only to meet specifications.
14. The fallacy of zero defects.
15. Inadequate testing of prototypes.
16. "Anyone who comes to try to help us must understand all about our business."

APPENDIX C

TYPICAL OUTPUT MEASUREMENTS

I.   Accounting Quality Measurements

1. Percent of late reports
2. Percent of errors in reports
3. Errors in input to information services
4. Errors reported by outside auditors
5. Percent of input errors detected
6. Number of complaints by users
7. Number of hours per week correcting or changing documents
8. Number of complaints about inefficiencies or excessive paper
9. Amount of time spent appraising/correcting input errors
10. Payroll processing time
11. Percent of errors in payroll
12. Length of time to prepare and send a bill
13. Length of time billed and not received
14. Number of final accounting jobs rerun
15. Number of equipment sales miscoded
16. Amount of intracompany accounting bill-back activity

17. Time spent correcting erroneous inputs
18. Number of open times
19. Percent of deviations from cash plan
20. Percent discrepancy in material review board and line scrap reports
21. Travel expense accounts processed in three days
22. Percent of advances outstanding
23. Percent data entry errors in accounts payable and general ledger
24. Credit turnaround time
25. Machine billing turnaround time
26. Percent of shipments requiring more than one attempt to invoice
27. Number of untimely supplier invoices processed
28. Average number of days from receipt to processing

II. Clerical Quality Measurements

1. Misfiles per week
2. Paper mailed/paper used
3. Errors per typed page
4. Administration errors (not using the right procedure)
5. Number of times manager is late to meetings
6. Number of times messages are not delivered
7. Percent of action items not done on schedule
8. Percent of inputs not received on schedule
9. Percent of coding errors on time cards
10. Period reports not completed on schedule
11. Percent of phone calls answered within two rings
12. Percent of phone calls dialed correctly
13. Error-free pages processed per hour
14. Clerical personnel/personnel supported
15. Percent of pages retyped
16. Percent of impressions reprinted

III. Product/Development Engineering Quality Measurements

 1. Percent of drafting errors per print
 2. Percent of prints released on schedule
 3. Percent of errors in cost estimates
 4. Number of times a print is changed
 5. Number of off-specs approved
 6. Simulation accuracy
 7. Accuracy of advance materials list
 8. Cost of input errors to the computer
 9. How well product meets customer expectations
10. Field performance of product
11. Percent of error-free designs
12. Percent of errors found during design review
13. Percent of repeat problems corrected
14. Time to correct a problem
15. Time required to make an engineering change
16. Cost of engineering changes per month
17. Percent of reports with errors in them
18. Data recording errors per month
19. Percent of evaluations that meet engineering objectives
20. Percent of special quotations that are successful
21. Percent of test plans that are changed (change/test plan)
22. Percent of meetings started on schedule
23. Spare parts' cost after warranty
24. Number of meetings held per quarter where quality and defect prevention were the main subject
25. Person-months per released print
26. Percent of total problems found by diagnostics as released
27. Customer cost per life of output delivered
28. Number of problems that were also encountered in previous products
29. Cycle time to correct a customer problem
30. Number of errors in publications reported from the plant and field

31. Number of products that pass independent evaluation error free
32. Number of missed shipments of prototypes
33. Number of unsuccessful preanalyses
34. Number of off-specs accepted
35. Percent of requests for engineering action for more than two weeks
36. Number of days late to preanalysis
37. Number of restarts of evaluations and tests
38. Effectiveness of regression tests
39. Number of days for the release cycle
40. Percent of corrective action schedules missed
41. Percent of bills of material that are released in error

IV.   Finance Quality Measurements

1. Percent error in budget predictions
2. Computer rerun time due to input errors
3. Computer program change cost
4. Percent of financial reports delivered on schedule
5. Number of record errors per employee
6. Percent of error-free vouchers
7. Percent of bills paid so company gets price break
8. Percent of errors in checks
9. Entry errors per week
10. Number of payroll errors per month
11. Number of errors in financial reports
12. Percent of errors in travel advancement records
13. Percent of errors in expense accounts detected by auditors

V.   Industrial/Plant Engineering

1. Percent of facilities on schedule
2. Percent of manufacturing time lost due to bad layouts
3. Percent of error in time estimates
4. Percent of error in purchase requests
5. Hours lost due to equipment downtime

    6. Scrap and rework due to calibration errors
    7. Repeat call hours for the same problem
    8. Changes to layout
    9. Percent deviation from budget
  10. Maintenance cost/equipment cost
  11. Number of errors found by outside auditors
  12. Number of unscheduled maintenance calls
  13. Number of hours used on unscheduled maintenance
  14. Number of hours used on scheduled maintenance
  15. Percent of equipment maintained on schedule
  16. Percent of equipment overdue for calibration
  17. Accuracy of assets report
  18. Percent of total floor space devoted to storage
  19. Number of industrial design completions past due
  20. Number of mechanical/functional errors in industrial design artwork
  21. Number of errors found after construction had been accepted by the company
  22. Percent of engineering action requests accepted

VI.   Forecasting Quality Measurements

    1. Number of upward pricing revisions per year
    2. Number of project plans that meet schedule, price, and quality
    3. Percent error in sales forecasts
    4. Number of forecasting assumption errors
    5. Number of changes in product schedules

VII.   Information Systems Quality Measurements

    1. Keypunch errors per day
    2. Input correction on CRT
    3. Reruns caused by operator error
    4. Percent of reports delivered on schedule
    5. Errors per thousand lines of code
    6. Number of changes after the program is coded

7. Percent of time required to debug programs
8. Rework costs resulting from computer programs
9. Number of cost estimates revised
10. Percent error in forecast
11. Percent error in lines of code required
12. Number of coding errors found during formal testing
13. Number of test case errors
14. Number of test case runs before success
15. Number of revisions to program objectives
16. Number of documentation errors
17. Number of revisions to program objectives
18. Number of errors found after formal test
19. Number of error-free programs delivered to customer
20. Number of process step errors before a correct package is ready
21. Number of revisions to checkpoint plan
22. Number of changes to customer requirements
23. Percent of programs not flow-diagrammed
24. Percent of customer problems not corrected per schedule
25. Percent of problems uncovered before design release
26. Percent change in customer satisfaction survey
27. Percent of defect-free artwork
28. System availability
29. Terminal response time
30. Mean time between system initial program loadings
31. Mean time between system repairs
32. Time before help calls are answered

VIII. Legal Quality Measurements

1. Response time on request for legal opinion
2. Time to prepare patent claims
3. Percent of cases lost

IX.   Management Quality Measurements

1. Security violations per year
2. Percent variation from budget
3. Percent of target dates missed
4. Percent of personnel turnover rate
5. Percent increase in output per employee
6. Percent absenteeism
7. Percent error in planning estimates
8. Percent of output delivered on schedule
9. Percent of employees promoted to better jobs
10. Department morale index
11. Percent of meetings that start on schedule
12. Percent of employee time spent on first-time output
13. Number of job improvement ideas per employee
14. Dollars saved per employee due to new ideas and/or methods
15. Ratio of direct to indirect employees
16. Increased percent of market
17. Return on investment
18. Percent of appraisals done on schedule
19. Percent of changes to project equipment required
20. Normal appraisal distribution
21. Percent of employee output that is measured
22. Number of grievances per month
23. Number of open doors per month
24. Percent of professional employees active in professional societies
25. Percent of managers active in community activities
26. Number of security violations per month
27. Percent of time program plans are met
28. Improvement in opinion surveys
29. Percent of employees who can detect and repair their own errors
30. Percent of delinquent suggestions

31. Percent of documents that require two management signatures
32. Percent error in personnel records
33. Percent of time cards signed by managers that have errors on them
34. Percent of employees taking higher education
35. Number of damaged equipment and property reports
36. Warranty costs
37. Scrap and rework costs
38. Cost of poor quality
39. Number of employees dropping out of classes
40. Number of decisions made by upper management than required by procedures
41. Improvement in customer satisfaction survey
42. Volume actual versus plan
43. Revenue actual versus plan
44. Number of formal reviews before plans are approved
45. Number of procedures with fewer than three acronyms and abbreviations
46. Percent of procedures fewer than 10 pages
47. Percent of employees active on improvement teams
48. Number of hours per year of career and skill development training per employee
49. Number of user complaints per month
50. Number of variances in capital spending
51. Percent revenue/expense ratio below plan
52. Percent of executive interviews with employees
53. Percent of departments with disaster recovery plans
54. Percent of appraisals with quality as a line item that makes up more than 30 percent of the evaluation
55. Percent of employees with development plans
56. Revenue generated over strategic period
57. Number of iterations of strategic plan
58. Number of employees participating in cost-effectiveness
59. Data integrity

60. Result of peer reviews
61. Number of tasks for which actual time exceeded estimated time

X. Manufacturing and Test Engineering Quality Measurements

1. Percent of process operations where sigma limit is within engineering specification
2. Percent of tools that fail certification
3. Percent of tools that are reworked due to design errors
4. Number of process changes for operation due to errors
5. In-process yields
6. Percent error in manufacturing costs
7. Time required to solve a problem
8. Number of delays because process instructions are wrong or not available
9. Labor utilization index
10. Percent error in test equipment and tooling budget
11. Number of errors in operator training documentation
12. Percent of errors that escape the operator's detections
13. Percent testers that fail certification
14. Percent error in yield projections
15. Percent error in output product quality
16. Asset utilization
17. Percent of designed experiments needing revision
18. Percent of changes to process specifications during process design review
19. Percent of equipment ready for production on schedule
20. Percent of meetings starting on schedule
21. Percent of drafting errors found by checkers
22. Percent manufacturing time used to screen products
23. Number of problems that the test equipment cannot detect during manufacturing cycle
24. Percent correlation between testers
25. Number of waivers to manufacturing procedures
26. Percent of tools and test equipment delivered on schedule

27. Percent of tools and test equipment on change level control
28. Percent functional test coverage of products
29. Percent projected cost reductions missed
30. Percent of action plan schedules missed
31. Equipment utilization

XI.   Manufacturing/Shipping Quality Measurements
1. Complaints on shipping damage
2. Percent of parts not packed to required specifications
3. Percent of output that meets customer orders and engineering specifications
4. Scrap and rework cost
5. Suggestions per employee
6. Percent of jobs that meet schedule
7. Percent of jobs that meet cost
8. Percent of defect-free product at measurement operations
9. Percent of employees trained to do the job they are working on
10. Accidents per month
11. Performance against standards
12. Percent of utilities left improperly running at end of shift
13. Percent unplanned overtime
14. Number of security violations per month
15. Percent of time log book filled out correctly
16. Time and/or claiming errors per week
17. Time between errors at each operation
18. Errors per 100,000 solder connections
19. Labor utilization index
20. Percent of operators certified to do their job
21. Percent of shipping errors
22. Defects during warranty period
23. Replacement parts defect rates
24. Percent of products defective at final test
25. Percent of control charts maintained correctly
26. Percent of invalid test data
27. Percent of shipments below plan
28. Percent of daily reports in by 7 A.M.

29. Percent late shipments
30. Percent of error-free products at final test

XII. Marketing Quality Measurements

1. Percent of proposals submitted ahead of schedule
2. Cost of sales per total costs
3. Percent error in marketing forecasts
4. Percent of proposals accepted
5. Percent of quota attained
6. Response time to customers inquiries
7. Inquiries per $10,000 of advertisement
8. Number of new customers
9. Percent of repeat orders
10. Percent of time customer expectations are identified
11. Sales made per call
12. Errors in orders
13. Ratio of marketing expenses to sales
14. Number of new business opportunities identified
15. Errors per contract
16. Percent of time customer expectation changes are identified before they impact sales
17. Man-hours per $10,000 sales
18. Percent reduction in residual inventory
19. Percent of customers called back as promised
20. Percent of meetings started on schedule
21. Number of complimentary letters
22. Percent of changed orders
23. Percent of phone numbers correctly dialed
24. Time required to turn in travel expense accounts
25. Number of revisions to market requirements statements per month
26. Percent of bids returned on schedule
27. Percent of customer letters answered in two weeks
28. Number of complaint reports received
29. Percent of complaint reports answered in three days

XIII. Personnel Quality Measurements

1. Percent of employees who leave during the first year
2. Number of days to answer suggestions
3. Number of suggestions resubmitted and approved
4. Personnel cost per employee
5. Percent of supplies delivered on schedule
6. Turnover rate due to poor performance
7. Number of grievances per month
8. Percent of employee requests filled on schedule
9. Number of days to fill an employment request
10. Management evaluation of management education courses
11. Time to process an applicant
12. Average time a visitor spends in the lobby
13. Time to get security clearance
14. Time to process insurance claims
15. Percent of employees participating in company-sponsored activities
16. Opinion survey ratings
17. Percent of complaints about salary
18. Percent of personnel problems handled by employee's managers
19. Percent of employees participating in voluntary health screening
20. Percent of offers accepted
21. Percent of retirees contacted yearly by phone
22. Percent of training classes evaluated as excellent
23. Percent deviation to resource plan
24. Wait time in medical department
25. Number of days to respond to applicant
26. Percent of promotions and management changes publicized
27. Percent of error-free newsletters

XIV. Procurement/Purchasing Quality Measurements

1. Percent of discount orders by consolidating
2. Errors per purchase order
3. Number of orders received with no purchase order
4. Routing and rate errors per shipment
5. Percent of supplies delivered on schedule
6. Percent decrease in parts cost
7. Expenditures per direct employee
8. Number of items on the hot list
9. Percent of suppliers with 100 percent lot acceptance for one year
10. Stock costs
11. Labor hours per $10,000 purchases
12. Purchase order cycle time
13. Number of times per year line is stopped due to lack of supplier parts
14. Supplier parts scrapped due to engineering changes
15. Percent of parts with two or more suppliers
16. Average time to fill emergency orders
17. Average time to replace rejected lots with good parts
18. Parts cost per total costs
19. Percent of lots received on line late
20. Actual purchased materials cost per budgeted cost
21. Time to answer customer complaints
22. Percent of phone calls dialed correctly
23. Percent of purchase orders returned due to errors or incomplete description
24. Percent of defect-free supplier model parts
25. Percent projected cost reductions missed
26. Time required to process equipment purchase orders
27. Cost of rush shipments
28. Number of items billed but not received

XV.   Production Control Quality Measurements

   1. Percent of late deliveries
   2. Percent of errors in stocking
   3. Number of items exceeding shelf life
   4. Percent of manufacturing jobs completed on schedule
   5. Time required to incorporate engineering changes
   6. Percent of errors in purchase requisitions
   7. Percent of products that meet customer orders
   8. Inventory turnover rate
   9. Time that line is down due to assembly shortage
  10. Percent of time parts are not in stock when ordered from common parts crib
  11. Time of product in shipment
  12. Cost of rush shipment
  13. Spare parts availability in crib
  14. Percent of errors in work-in-process records versus audit data
  15. Cost of inventory spoilage
  16. Number of bill-of-lading errors not caught in shipping

XVI.   Quality Assurance Quality Measurements

   1. Percent error in reliability projections
   2. Percent of errors in stocking
   3. Time to answer customer complaints
   4. Number of customer complaints
   5. Number of errors detected during design and process reviews
   6. Percent of employees active in professional societies
   7. Number of audits performed on schedule
   8. Percent of quality assurance personnel to total personnel
   9. Percent of quality inspectors to manufacturing directs
  10. Percent of quality engineers to product and manufacturing engineers
  11. Number of engineering changes after design review
  12. Number of process changes after design review

13. Errors in reports
14. Time to correct a problem
15. Cost of scrap and rework that was not created at the rejected operation
16. Percent of suppliers at 100 percent lot acceptance for one year
17. Percent of lots going directly to stock
18. Percent of problems identified in the field
19. Variations between inspectors doing the same jobs
20. Percent of reports published on schedule
21. Number of complaints from manufacturing management
22. Percent of field returns correctly analyzed
23. Time to identify and solve problems
24. Percent of laboratory services not completed on schedule
25. Percent of improvement in early detection of major design errors
26. Percent of errors in defect records
27. Number of reject orders not dispositioned in five days
28. Number of customer calls to report errors
29. Level of customer surveys
30. Number of committed supplier plans in place
31. Percent of correlated test results with suppliers
32. Receiving inspection cycle time
33. Number of requests for corrective action being processed
34. Time required to process a request for corrective action
35. Number of off-specs approved
36. Percent of part numbers going directly to stock
37. Number of manufacturing interruptions caused by supplier parts
38. Percent error in predicting customer performance
39. Percent product cost related to appraisal, scrap, and rework
40. Percent skip lot inspection
41. Percent of qualified suppliers
42. Number of problems identified in-process

XVII. Security/Safety Quality Measurements

1. Percent of clearance errors
2. Time to get clearance
3. Percent of security violations
4. Percent of documents classified incorrectly
5. Security violations per audit
6. Percent of audits conducted on schedule
7. Percent of safety equipment checked per schedule
8. Number of safety problems identified by management versus total safety problems identified
9. Safety accidents per 100,000 hours worked
10. Safety violations by department
11. Number of safety suggestions
12. Percent of sensitive parts located

This list was derived from a more complete outline provided by Harrington.

Be careful with many of the processes just listed and their corresponding variables. For many of these, a temporary control chart versus a permanent real-time type would be recommended for analysis purposes. Sometimes historical data will reveal the important issues:

1. Is the variable in-control?
2. What is the process capability?
3. Can local faults be categorized or Pareto-ized?
4. Are interdepartmental teams necessary?

ENDNOTES

1. M. Detouzous, R. Lester, and R. Solow. *Made in America: Regaining the Productive Edge.* Cambridge, MA: The MIT Commission on Industrial Productivity, MIT Press, 1990: 10.
2. R. Pascale and A. Athos. *The Art of Japanese Management.* New York: Warner Books, 1981: 131.
3. W. Ouchi. *The M-Form Society.* Reading, PA: Addison-Wesley, 1984: 4.
4. D. Halberstam. *The Reckoning.* New York: Avon Books, 1986: 49.
5. A. V. Feigenbaum. "Quality and Productivity." *Quality Progress* (November 1977): 18-23.
6. M. Walton. *The Deming Management Method.* New York: Perigee Books, 1986: 134.
7. R. Levering. *A Great Place to Work.* New York: Random House, 1988: 261.
8. G. P. Fellers. *SPC for Practitioners: Special Cases and Continuous Processes.* Milwaukee: ASQC Quality Press, 1991.
9. W. E. Deming. *Out of the Crisis.* Cambridge, MA: MIT Center for Advanced Engineering Study, 1986: 7, 463, 33.
10. J. Ryan. "The Human Side of Quality." American Society for Quality Control Brochure, Milwaukee: ASQC, 1990: 6.
11. W. Latzko. "Reducing Clerical Costs." In *Annual Technical Quality Transactions.* Milwaukee: ASQC, 1974: 37.
12. F. Larson and F. LaFasto. *Teamwork.* Newbury Park, CA: Sage Publications, 1989: 37, 115.

13. J. Naisbitt and P. Aburdene. *Reinventing the Corporation.* New York: Warner Books, 1986: 38.
14. H. Artinian and E. Baker. "The Case of Windsor Export Supply." *Quality Progress* (June 1985): 65.
15. H. Gitlow and S. Gitlow. *The Deming Guide to Quality and Competitive Position.* Englewood Cliffs, NJ: Prentice-Hall, 1987: 48.
16. H. J. Harrington. *Excellence the IBM Way.* Milwaukee: ASQC Quality Press, 1988: 95-106.
17. H. Lefevre. *Quality Service Pays: Six Keys to Success.* Milwaukee: ASQC Quality Press, 1989: 50, 181, 268.
18. *Car and Driver* (August 1983): 3.
19. T. Peters and R. Waterman, Jr. *Thriving on Chaos.* New York: Alfred A. Knoff Publishers, 1987: 91.
20. R. K. Dobbins. "Quality Cost and Profit Performance. In *Annual Quality Conference Transactions.* Milwaukee: ASQC, 1978: 75.
21. T. Peters and R. Waterman, Jr. *In Search of Excellence.* New York: Harper & Row, 1982: 172.
22. W. Scherkenbach. *The Deming Route to Quality and Productivity.* Milwaukee: ASQC Quality Press, 1987: 30.
23. H. Neave. *The Deming Dimension.* Knoxville, TN: SPC Press, 1990: 364.
24. M. Ray and R. Myers. *Creativity in Business.* New York: Doubleday, 1989: 164, 401.
25. M. P. Demos. "SQC's Role in Healthcare Management." *Quality Progress* (August 1989): 85-89.
26. "Catch a Falling Star." *U.S. News & World Report* (June 5, 1989): 43-44.
27. M. McLean, G. Preston, and K. Jillson. "The Manager and Self-Respect." New York: AMA Survey Report, AMACOM, 1975: 2.
27. R. Moen. "The Performance Appraisal System: Deming's Deadly Disease." *Quality Progress* (November 1989): 62-66.
28. W. McCabe. "Quality Methods Applied to the Business Process." In *Annual Quality Congress Transactions.* Milwaukee: ASQC, 1986: 433.

29. "Today's Leaders Look to Tomorrow." *Fortune* (March 26, 1990).

30. T. Deal and A. Kennedy. *Corporate Cultures.* New York: Addison-Wesley, 1982: 93.

31. M. Mobley. "Marketing Research and the Manufacturing Process." In *News & Views*. Augusta, GA: Augusta College School of Business Administration, Fall 1988: 1.

32. G. Taguchi and D. Clausing. "Robust Quality." *Harvard Business Review* (January-February 1990): 65.

33. W. E. Deming. *Quality, Productivity, and Competitive Position.* Cambridge, MA: MIT Center for Advanced Engineering Study, 1982: 30.

34. G. Kuretz. "The Acquisition Boom Has Lost a Lot of Its Thunder." *Business Week* (June 12, 1989): 234.

35. F. Luthans and K. Thompson. "Theory D and Organization Behavior Modification: Synergistic or Opposite Approaches to Performance Improvement." In *Organizational Behavior Management and Statistical Process Control,* edited by Thomas C. Mawhenny. New York: Hawthorne Press, 1987: 109-119.

INDEX